SIMPLY WILDE

By Stuart Wilde

Books

THE TAOS QUINTET:

Affirmations
The Force
Miracles
The Quickening
The Trick to Money Is Having Some!

* * *

Infinite Self: 33 Steps to Reclaiming Your Inner Power
"Life Was Never Meant to Be a Struggle"
The Little Money Bible
The Secrets of Life
Silent Power
Simply Wilde
Weight Loss for the Mind
Whispering Winds of Change

Audiocassettes

The Art of Meditation
The Force (audio book)
Happiness Is Your Destiny
Intuition
Loving Relationships
Miracles (audio book)
Silent Power (audio book)

SIMPLY WILDE

DISCOVER THE WISDOM THAT IS

Stuart Wilde

with Leon Nacson

Hay House, Inc.
Carlsbad, CA

Published and distributed in the United States by:
Hay House, Inc., P.O. Box 5100, Carlsbad, CA 92018-5100
(800) 654-5126 • (800) 650-5115 (fax)

Edited by: Leigh Robshaw, Anna Scott, and Jill Kramer
Designed by: Rhett Nacson and Wendy Lutge

Library of Congress Cataloging-in-Publication Data

Wilde, Stuart
Simply Wilde : discover the wisdom that is / Stuart Wilde : with Leon Nacson.
p. cm.
Originally published: Sydney, Australia : Nacson & Sons, 1998.
ISBN 1-56170-620-5 (trade paper)
1. Conduct of life—Miscellanea. I. Nacson, Leon. II. Title.
BJ1581.2.W523 1999
131—dc21 98-29184
CIP

Originally published in 1998 by Nacson & Sons, Sydney, Australia

ISBN 1-56170-620-5

02 01 00 99 4 3 2 1

First Hay House Printing, April 1999
2nd Printing, April 1999

Printed in Canada

For Sebastien,
Rhett, Eli & Joanne

CONTENTS

FOREWORD

I have always been intrigued by Stuart Wilde and his philosophy, so I was delighted a few years ago when the opportunity arose to publish his work in the USA. His books and tapes quickly became a popular feature of the Hay House catalog: It seems that many people, like myself, feel drawn to this truly unique character and his empowering teachings.

This book is particularly courageous in that Stuart openly and honestly discusses many of today's delicate subjects, such as politics, sex, drugs, abortion, and homosexuality. It is overflowing with Stuart's profound wisdom and his brilliant insights into spirituality and metaphysics. Also, sprinkled throughout are anecdotes about Stuart's personal life. What a combination for entertaining and impactful reading!

As you delve into this colorful tapestry of thoughts, you'll find answers to questions that you, his readers, have asked—questions that have baffled you and questions to which you can personally relate.

As Stuart Wilde's American publisher, I can testify to the amount of mail and inquiries we receive each week about Stuart and his work. I'm sure that *Simply Wilde* will excite many of his fans, offering as it does a rare insight into the man himself. And, because it presumes no previous knowledge of his concepts, it's an ideal vehicle for new seekers to explore his work for the first time.

It pleases me greatly that my dear friends Stuart Wilde and Leon Nacson have teamed up to produce this wonderful new book.

My fondest memories of Stuart are of our 1994 tour of Australia with Wayne Dyer, Marianne Williamson, and Michael Rowlands. For me it was a challenging tour as we traveled to every capital city in Australia. But sharing the program with Stuart lightened the load. He was a treasure to be with, enlivening every day with his peculiar brand of charm and offbeat humor.

I was also happy to catch up with Leon Nacson on the tour. I'll always remember the way he looked after me, especially during those long hours of book signings and photographs. He was always by my side with water and fruit to feed my body, and flowers to feed my soul.

Simply Wilde deals with something we all have an interest in—Life! But be warned: Stuart's perspective on life is not always what we expect.

Whether or not you agree with Stuart Wilde's perceptions, however, you can't deny that he is one of a kind. To me, that is a very endearing quality indeed.

—LOUISE L. HAY

ACKNOWLEDGMENTS

A big thanks to Leigh Robshaw for ensuring that this book was actually completed. We could not have done it without your persistent hours of researching, collating, and editing. Thanks to the other members of our editorial team, Rachel Eldred and Claudia Blaxell. To our senior editor Anna Scott, you have done a superb job once again.

INTRODUCTION

It was springtime of '83 and I was about to participate in Stuart Wilde's first Australian seminar. Glynn Braddy, Australian health researcher and philosopher, had spoken about his dear friend Stuart Wilde for the past three months, so I was looking forward to meeting him. Glynn introduced us, and with that first handshake, I embarked on a 15-year adventure as Stuart's Australian promoter and publisher.

Stuart lived up to all that had been said about him. We had heard that Stuart was a charismatic and empowering speaker, but no one had expected his workshop to be so much fun. Stuart was, and still is, a seriously funny guy. We came for a shot of metaphysics, and got much more than we'd bargained for. By the end of the day, we were rolling on the floor, tears of laughter streaming down our cheeks. Stuart has the knack of combining metaphysics and spirituality with entertainment and humor, and that's what makes him unique.

There was a portion of the workshop that covered one's attitude to money. Stuart announced with a cheeky grin: "The guy who wrote that 'money is the root of all evil' just flat out didn't have any." I remember thinking, *This guy's okay*. That one daring phrase changed my abundance consciousness and my attitudes toward money forever.

I'll never forget the first time I heard the term *tick-tock*, which is Stuart's term for the humdrum rhythm of a 9-to-5 life. It was amusing to witness everyone work it into their vocabulary almost immediately. From then on it was "tick-tock this" and "tick-tock that," "here a tick, there a tock, everywhere a tick-tock." It was my first indication of Stuart's ability to coin a simple but catchy phrase that could perfectly capture the nature of something so intangible. In fact, Stuart's gift has always been to take ideas, theories, and philosophies previously thought of as too esoteric for the average person to comprehend and teach them in a simple, straightforward, and, of course, humorous way.

Over the years I have published 11 of Stuart's books, and we have conducted some unforgettable workshops and seminars. People still talk about the first Warrior's Wisdom course. At this highly impacting intensive, Stuart taught people how to live life and face death.

At that first Warrior's Wisdom seminar, we were to rappel down the cliffs at Manly in Sydney, Australia. Now these are dangerously high cliffs, and we had nothing but air and a tiny little rope between us and the white sand way below. In the group were grandmothers, grandfathers, teenagers, a pregnant woman, and even a gentleman with one arm. Every last one of them faced their fears and descended that cliff. Not far from us was a group of professionals all decked out in their jazzy gear. The leader asked me how long we'd been practicing, and to his disbelief I told him it was our first time. Most of our group had never been this close to a cliff edge in their lives. He thought we were crazy. Perhaps we were. There is a quote from an old French poem by Guillaume Apollinaire in one of Stuart's first books that captures the essence of that workshop:

Come to the cliff, he said.
They said, we are afraid.
Come to the cliff, he said.
They came.
He pushed them.
And they flew.

The Warrior's Wisdom course eventually became the acclaimed Warriors in the Mist seminar. Last year Stuart conducted his final Warriors in the Mist in Taos, New Mexico, and decided to concentrate on writing rather than public speaking for the time being. But that hasn't stopped people from calling me to ask when Stuart's next seminar will take place. Whenever I bring up the subject, Stuart's answer is always the same: "As soon as I have something new to say, I'll be there."

This brings me to "the house." Stuart decided to build a small adobe-style house in a secluded valley south of Sydney so that he and his son, Sebastien, would have somewhere cool to hang out during school holidays. However, Stuart does not do things by halves. What has evolved is no house—it's a castle. In fact, it's the first of three Tolemac castles that Stuart is manifesting as part of his new teaching. As many of you know, Tolemac is the name of Stuart's company. (If you print the word *TOLEMAC* on a sheet of paper and hold it up to a mirror, you'll see where the word comes from.)

The first castle in the Tolemac trio is a place that challenges your beliefs and encourages you to look deep inside yourself. Some of the doorways are built so low that you are forced to stoop to enter, a reminder that the ego must also stoop and be subjugated if we are to cross the threshold and enter higher levels of consciousness. And what of the empty room with no doors and no windows? You can't enter and you can't leave. Its purpose is a mystery each person must solve for themselves. It's like the massive boulder that dominates the main bathroom, which was so huge that it had to be lowered in through the roof with a crane. Why go to so much trouble for what seems like a fairly ordinary rock? "Just so that people can sit in the bathroom wondering what this big rock is doing there," says Stuart. Nothing can be taken for granted in the Tolemac castle. The assumptions you make in your everyday life cannot accompany you into the castle because here, things are never what they seem.

Sanctuaries of silence, meditation, and contemplation are sprinkled throughout the castle. There is a

Japanese bathhouse for steam baths, meditation, and tea ceremonies. Running throughout the building and into the forest are 500 feet of secret tunnels and passages that beckon the spiritual traveler to explore the unknown. The castle exudes Stuart's energy, and you can feel his presence throughout the building. In a way, it embodies many of Stuart's greatest qualities —strength, exuberance, generosity, originality, distinction, abundance, and mystery.

The trio of Tolemac castles will manifest at certain energy points in the earth when the time is right. The energy has already begun to build as the new millennium draws closer. The Tolemac castles appeared to Stuart in a vision as centers of spiritual learning in the tradition of Camelot. Entering the castles will be like entering another dimension, where love, healing, peace, wisdom, freedom, and solidarity reign. As the evolution of the Tolemac progresses, individuals from every corner of the planet will feel the calling, know that their time has come, and step bravely up to take their place in a dimension of higher consciousness.

While he awaits the transformation of the Tolemac energy, Stuart is busy writing books and music. His latest book, *The Little Money Bible,* is already a great success, as are his three CDs, *Cecilia—Voice of the Feminine Spirit*, *Cecilia—Voice of Violet 19,* and *Greenwood—Voice of the Celtic Myth.* As Stuart is traveling a lot less than he used to—the record was 90 cities in 164 days—we decided it would be the perfect time to compile this book.

Over the years we have been inundated with people wanting to know more about Stuart and his work. There have been endless seminar questions, phone calls, letters, and, more recently, e-mails to Stuart's website. We've had a great time choosing our favorite questions from among the multitudes. We hope you find just as much enjoyment in reading them. Now, fellow fringe dwellers, let's see why Stuart Wilde is known as the "teacher's teacher."

—LEON NACSON

Chapter One

WILDE ABOUT LIFE

What is our purpose here on the Earth plane?

The whole object of this Earth journey is for us to develop spiritual freedom and to develop an understanding of ourselves—to go beyond fear and restriction and to express yourself in a dimension that is deliberately designed to control you. I believe we are very heroic beings, because there are trillions and trillions of spirits that wouldn't bloody come here if you gave them all the tea in China. We are the pioneers of this incredible experience, trying to win our freedom within the confusion of regulations, social ideas, sexual stereotypes, religious and political dogma, and the military machines that are running our world. If you feel a little inadequate, if you feel somewhat frightened or insecure, if you feel slightly pissed off, if you don't really see the path—don't worry; that is actually how it's supposed to be.

Imagine coming to a dimension where you were honored, and those already there gave you tea and biscuits and said, "Here's a couple of million dollars to get on with this incarnation. Why don't you have a farm with 60 acres and a perfect body?" You wouldn't come, would you? It would be like looking at a crossword puzzle with all the letters filled in. So, it's the very fact that you haven't got a clue what you're doing here that makes you heroic, and which makes the journey worthwhile.

I work really hard to stay mentally, emotionally, and physically balanced. I keep various disciplines yet sometimes find that imbalance creeps up on me without warning. Why do these slips occur, and how can I prevent them?

The more you raise your energy—the more you work on yourself to control the mental, emotional, and physical self; the more rarefied your diet, the more rarefied your consciousness—the harder it is to sustain discipline. If you are finding it really difficult to maintain a balance, an effective technique is to deliberately lower your energy. There are times when the energy gets so intense that it keeps falling off the shelf. Probably at that point what you really need to do is eat a little crud, drink a little alcohol, basically give up on the disciplines for a bit, and slip back to a place where your energy is easily sustained.

In the early days, I found that as my metaphysical energy was increasing and I was concentrating on the power of the Light, I would get overwhelmed by energy and wouldn't know what to do with it. A lot of my imbalance occurred because I was rather spastic in the way I accommodated energy. We tend to take on much more energy than we ever need.

So, in answer to your question, sometimes the slips happen through lack of concentration. But, more often than not, it's because you have too much energy and things get wobbly and out of control. That's when it's time to pull back.

In step seven of your book and tape series *Infinite Self: 33 Steps to Reclaiming Your Inner Power*, you talk about guilt as a great human weakness. I was brought up in a family where I was made to feel guilty for everything, and find it difficult to transcend this deep-seated emotion. How would you suggest I banish guilt from my life—not just on an intellectual level, but on a deep emotional level?

I think guilt and shame are two of the hardest emotions to go beyond because they usually come from the family of origin, and therefore from one's upbringing. Even though they are emotions that come from an opinion, the opinions are entrenched very deeply. If someone was shamed as a child, you can't just say to the person, "Let go of the shame," because the shame is a profound part of who they are. So with shame and guilt, I think you need the assistance of a qualified counselor who can talk you through your inner-child experience. You can then begin to see how you took on those experiences in childhood, and that it was part of your evolution and how you dealt with growing up.

I believe the higher self has a vision of what it's going to be up to each lifetime. You accepted your family and their weaknesses. When they put guilt and shame upon you, they were usually expressing their own insecurity. Even though they may have been bastards, they were bastards because they were taught weakness by somebody else. It's quite a heroic thing for you to break the chain so that this isn't handed down to your children.

I try so hard to be a success in life, but I seem to attract more failure than success. When I am successful, I can't accept it; and when I fail, I beat myself up about it.

One of my favorite quotes was written by me: "Life: never take it personally." If you can get to a point where you don't take it personally, you are recognizing that you are a spirit, a golden light inside a funny little physical body. And inside the physical body is a funny little personality that really hasn't got a clue, and a funny little ego that needs nurturing. That's what we are, just funny little people playing a game inside this thing called life. So, when you look at the contrast of the ego and the spirit, you can see that it is only a matter of controlling your personality, and the first point of your control is deciding that you are not going to be the personality. In other words, are you that person? Are you your emotions? Are you your anguish? Are you your pain? Are you your success, your failure? You're not. And if you think you are, I feel sorry for you. You have a long, hard, painful journey ahead. You arc a divine spirit, don't forget that.

How can I be free from the negative and fearful thoughts and emotions that dominate me?

Don't let yourself become a victim of your emotions. When you are scared, it isn't the real you that is scared, it is your personality interpreting circumstances that may be adverse. You are not these emotions; they don't own you. As you begin to understand that you don't belong to your emotions, then you can detach from them. It's simply a matter of saying, "I won't be victimized by my emotions."

Don't make the mistake of confusing your emotions with your feelings. Your feelings are inside the etheric. They are 500,000 times faster than you think they are. They are quick, they can move anywhere, they can look at anything. What you think are your feelings are just emotional or physical sensations, and for the most part, they are crawling along at very slow speeds. You are not these emotions. When you are scared, your personality and ego lead you to believe that you are the fear. But you can't be. It's impossible for that to happen to you. You exist as a spirit beyond these things.

If you have reconciled fear, you are free. If you accept your life, you are free. If you don't resist, you are free. It's only the ego that says you have to have a pain-free existence. It's only the ego that says you shouldn't die. It's only the ego that says you have to have glamour and importance. It's only the ego that says you have to follow the path that it wants you to follow. It's nonsense. Life will go the way it goes. And when you don't fight it, you're free. The less you fight it, the less anguish and negativity you create.

When you think about it, there is no negative energy upon our Earth plane. We live in a 100 percent positive dimension, a pure dimension of spirituality and goodness. The only form of negative energy we can experience amounts to nothing more than contradictions of the ego's opinions. If your ego believes you should be immortal and you drop dead, it's a contradiction. If your ego believes you should not experience pain and you hit your thumb with a hammer, it's a contradiction. In fact, if you didn't have an ego parliament inside your head, you could not experience negativity.

Animals live in an absolutely positive dimension. Even if an animal breaks a leg and is in pain, it doesn't think, *My God, this is ghastly.* It doesn't have a concept of ghastly. It doesn't have an opinion that says a broken leg is worse than a healthy leg. It has pain sensations running up its leg, but it doesn't have an opinion that resists the experience. So as you give away the resistance and reconcile death, and as you understand the incredible heroism and beauty of this existence, you can free yourself from all emotions.

When I talk about thoughts and feelings, confusion arises and I find that they clash. Confusion is something I have to deal with a lot. Where does confusion come from?

It comes directly from the ego and the personality: "Shall I, shall I not? Is it right, is it wrong? Am I okay, am I not okay?" Once you don't ask any questions, you can't be confused. You need to use the intellect in order to be confused. There is no other way of doing it. Once you dominate the intellect and don't allow it to ask too many questions, you are totally free. So don't ask questions. If it feels right, it is right. If it doesn't feel right, it is either not necessary at this precise moment, or it is not right. Just go with your intuition, go with your sensitivity, and you will be fine.

How can I control anger? I meditate often and am generally a peaceful person, but sometimes anger rises and I become overwhelmed by it.

Just don't be angry. You might say, "Well, that's easy enough to say, Stuart; I'm really pissed off." Don't be. What is anger? It's only a game. Something has come along and contradicted your ego—that's all that has happened. Anger comes from loss. To generate the emotion of anger, you will have to have lost something. There is no other way for anger to rise. Perhaps you've lost your importance, security, wallet, romance, job? When you are really pissed off, take a moment to figure out what you have lost. Sure enough, it will be there. Loss of prestige, loss of rhythm, loss of a promise, loss of a dream—loss of many things that you probably didn't need anyway. Once you notice what you've lost, the next move for a spiritual person is to absolutely, categorically agree to lose it. Rather than taking the loss personally, engaging the ego, and talking about justice and rights, just shrug and acknowledge what has happened. When you don't resist, you are free.

There are certain circumstances where you might feel you should chase after what you have lost, but 99 percent of the time it is incredibly futile. When you lose things, it's only the God force being kind to you. It's liberating you from stuff you honestly don't need. Think how many times you've been in a relationship in which the person left and you went absolutely crazy. You couldn't breathe, you couldn't eat, life wasn't worth living. A week later it felt different. Three months later somebody says, "What happened to whatshisname?" and you say, "Who?"

The other thing to remember about anger is that much of it comes from your early childhood. The dysfunctions, abuse, abandonment, and mistreatment that we suffer in our early years stays with us. The only real way to become a complete person is to look at the pain and the suffering, and release that anger. Sometimes it's useful to bang cushions or to talk to a therapist, but you can never be completely free of anger unless you go back to those things that are very deeply programmed inside of you—the things that caused you hurt, pain, guilt, and resentment in your early years.

Although I am fairly confident, I occasionally experience incredible feelings of insecurity. I don't find it very pleasant and wish I could stop feeling this way.

Insecurity is easy to deal with. How? Don't fight it. Isn't it true, when we fight legal battles or wars, the situation becomes more important by the very fact that we are concentrating on it? This is an insecure dimension for the ego. So when you begin to feel insecure, say to yourself, "Of course I do, ducky, that's part of what's going on here." When you're scared, rather than believing in the fear, stand to one side and say, "Yes, of course I'm scared. This is an insecure place." It's only the law of the ego that says you can't be scared. Just accept and love yourself for your weaknesses.

Then again, as I said in response to the question on anger, insecurity comes from your childhood. When you are scared and you feel the loss of life force through your navel, or the anger in your gut, it's useful to concentrate upon that area of your physical body and ask yourself, "How old am I?" If what scares you is not in your present circumstances, it's very likely that life is triggering a reaction, and you might find that your gut tells you, "You are four years old." Then you can go back to that point in your life and see that the insecurity or fear was created by circumstances in your childhood, in the context of your family of origin.

How do we decrease pain in our lives? I can understand the idea of not succumbing to ego or negative thoughts, but pain is something I find difficult to deal with. Can we ever be free of pain?

First, have absolutely no consideration or attitude about how long the pain is going to last. In other words, you're not going to come from the ego's perspective of, "God, I hope this is over quickly . . . how long can I stand it . . . will I make it . . . ?" Don't take it personally and don't see it as an affront to your security, stability, or your desire to establish control. Don't let the ego resist by allowing it to ask why. Just stop fighting the pain and it won't feel so bad. Pain is the classroom of the evolving external spirit. Remember that. Say, "I'm in school today!"

To experience extreme levels of pain, you have to have extreme levels of resistance. Get rid of the legislation, "I should be living a pain-free existence," and you're free. That is what the fringe dwellers will teach people—that they are not the emotion, they're not the frustration, they're not the anguish, they're not the pain, and there is no lack. We are love, temporarily solidified.

I sometimes feel sad about the state of my life, and I feel I should have achieved more by now.

The only sadness in this world would be if you reached your last day on the Earth plane and you had never *lived*, if you had spent your life just paying off a mortgage on a little house in the suburbs that eventually became your prison. The ego believes this is security. And in the end, if you step back and look at this little place, it's four little bricks in the suburbs with a few grotty little flying ducks over the mantelpiece. That isn't security, that's a prison. It's a prison you spent all your life looking after, all your life working for. For the most part, it's nonsense. Most of you don't need it. If you feel you do need it and you have enough money, then buy it. But most of us spend our whole life working to pay off a house, then when we die, the kids sell the house and bugger off to the south of France. If you're sad about your life, why not sell the little house in the suburbs, find a toy boy and bugger off to the south of France before you die? If someone asks you what you're doing, tell them you are on a spiritual evolution.

You say that creative pursuits will enhance spirituality, but how can I enhance my creativity?

Creativity comes about by actually doing something creative. Most people are too inhibited to get started, or they do a little bit and then give up.

The best thing you can do to enhance your creativity is develop the discipline to do a little bit every day. It may mean you have to get up at four o'clock in the morning and do an hour of writing, music, painting, sewing, woodwork, or whatever your creative pursuit might be. It's in the doing that you get in touch with the God Force within, the higher self within. It's that connection that enables you to reach the height of creativity. Even if you can only do ten minutes, try to do it every day.

Step 14 of *Infinite Self: 33 Steps to Reclaiming Your Inner Power*, is Judge Nothing, Quantify Nothing. I try so hard not to judge people, but I just can't help myself. It seems like a primal urge that I can't control. I wonder if not judging anyone is actually going against human nature?

I agree that nonjudgment is almost unnatural. It's part of our survival mechanism to evaluate, and in evaluating, we judge. As somebody walks down the street toward us, we evaluate whether they're going to eat us or whether we're going to eat them. We're evaluating whether they're a predator, a supporter, or neutral.

However, in order to touch the spiritual self, you have to go deep inside your subliminal fears, hatreds, and antagonisms to clean them out. You can work on an intellectual level by not voicing too many criticisms and judgments, and not being nasty to people. You can work on an emotional level by not abusing people, taking advantage of them, threatening them, or manipulating them. You can control yourself on a physical level by not physically abusing people. But in the end, you also have to possess in the deep inner core of your spirituality a love for humankind.

All judgment comes from insecurity, from the need to put people down or lessen their importance. We find it comfortable to box people into some position so we can feel we are worth more, and can therefore feel more secure, more loved, more observed, more special. Something to remember about judgment and criticism is that these feelings will arise when you're tired and irritable. Most people have their need to judge under control, but when you observe the shadow side of yourself being expressed, the important thing is to take time to release it. Maybe you need to punch the pillows on the bed, or visualize telling a person how angry you are with them. It's good to express that shadow side in harmless ways so it doesn't need to be acted out by way of real criticism, arguments, or fights. The answer is just do the best you can.

In your tape series *Assertiveness*, you say, "In my philosophy, anything that is not individual or original has no use." You've said in other works that we should call on the energy of successful people in our creative fields, but if I do that, am I still being original?

I don't think I was talking about individuality or originality in an absolutely strict sense. Naturally one has to build on what has gone before in order to create the individuality that one seeks. I think that too often people fall back on just parroting or copying what has already been done. I think it is important to try to be original without being silly. You don't have to be very different, just slightly different. It is helpful to be familiar with experts and other successful people in your field, because it gives you groundwork to build upon. But it would seem that these two aspects, taken out of context, tend to contradict each other here. If there is any contradiction, I apologize. I certainly didn't mean it to be that way.

I've been receiving therapy for several years and sometimes wonder if I'm getting anywhere. How do you know when to persevere and when it's time to cut your losses and get on with life?

Therapy is valuable because it allows you to go and talk to a professional about the intimate details of your life, rather than spilling out your problems to your friends who may not be able to advise you so well. However, there is a point in therapy where you reach a diminishing return. In other words, in order to talk about your pain, you have to engage the personality/ego. There is nothing that the personality/ego likes better than waffling on about itself and having somebody say, "There, there." Quite naturally, a therapist can't say to you, "Listen, you're full of shit; you're an egotistical, arrogant bastard, and what you really need to do is cut the crap and get out there, roll up your sleeves, and get on with your life." That would automatically put the therapist out of a job, but that is actually what a lot of people need to hear.

A lot of therapy is so indulgent and goes on for years because the client needs to have the attention, and the therapist needs to work. I think when you feel bored by the therapy, when you feel you're going back over the same stuff, when you see that there really isn't any more to be gained from it, that's the time to cut your losses and get on with your life. If someone has been seeing a therapist for more than six months on a weekly basis and still hasn't figured it out, then really, it's time to trash the therapist and get on with it.

I find it difficult to cope with all the contradictions of life—for example, trying to become a more spiritual and peaceful person in an increasingly violent and materialistic world.

Life is a paradox. We are required to believe in a God we cannot see. We are required to accept and embrace love on a planet where there is so much hatred. We are required to accept abundance when everybody tells you there isn't enough. We're required to see beauty where there is a lot of ugliness. We're required to embrace balance when we see people conking out and dropping left, right, and center. We're required to try to embrace peace and serenity when all you see on television is violence. So yes, there are many contradictions—but that's what makes it beautiful.

Chapter Two

WILDE ABOUT ENLIGHTENMENT

Why do you think so many people have such a big problem with truth?

The reason people have such a problem with truth is really a matter of two things: self-image and security. Let me explain this to you in terms of the etheric. The etheric is the bio-electric energy field or life force that emanates from the physical body. A person who has a weak etheric doesn't have a strong sense of self. They have been squashed down in life, victimized, abused, or perhaps they've just never experienced being a successful person. They will feel overwhelmed by circumstances, they will always feel they are underperforming, and they will place themselves below everyone else. They might walk into a restaurant and feel shy as people look at them walking to their table. At parties or in the company of other people, they will place themselves lower, or judge themselves in light of the people around them.

Because of that insecurity and poor self-image, people have to compensate. When you meet a person who is a typical babbling brook: "Yak, yak, yak, I've done this, I've experienced that," they are trying to cover up their poor self-image, poor self-worth, and fear. They are covering up the fact that they are scared.

So, entering the truth of who you are, the silence within, is an incredibly holy, spiritual, and courageous thing to do. It is about accepting yourself as no more than what you are at this point in time. There is an incredible spiritual power in accepting who you are, knowing, of course, that you can strengthen yourself at a later date.

You talk about people being afraid of moving into the unknown. How important is change in a person's life?

Naturally we are scared to move into the unknown because our personality relies a lot on the symbols, psychological structures, and associations we develop. We become comfortable in a society, and with a group of people—work mates, family, and friends. However, embracing change is a matter of giving away or letting go of old traits. It's all a matter of lowering your resistance and trusting. You can't become something more if you can't let go of where you find yourself today.

Change is perpetual. One way of evaluating your spirituality is by the freedom and looseness that you enjoy. It's the concept of being ready for perpetual change, for change means that your energy is oscillating quickly, your life is fresh, and you are in an expanding evolution.

The ego/personality likes to create rhythm and structure. It seeks to hold you in place, where it can feel safe, where you can develop associations, observers, status, and importance. The ego likes to nail you down. It doesn't like anything unexpected happening. Boring and stale feels safe to the ego.

The spiritual traveler moves at speed, holding on to very little, tolerating their challenges, and accepting life as they find it. Moving into the unknown is a matter of melting the resistance that one has to change, taking responsibility, and being able to accept that nothing is permanent and it doesn't have to be for you to feel secure. For in the end, we will all change and melt into something bigger and better. That's the nature of the spiritual journey, and that's pretty cool in my view. Give yourself away today to become something more tomorrow.

How important is it to avoid indecision?

Ernest Holmes wrote: "Where your mind goes, energy flows." If you're indecisive, you are putting out messages that say, "I don't know what I want." So life reflects back to you the same message, saying, "If you don't know, mate, who the hell does?"

Either act with clarity, courage, and conviction; or sit still, wait, and do not act. There's a right time for everything. Sometimes it's more powerful to do nothing or to retreat than it is to advance. When it feels right, act—and act decisively and powerfully. I think that a lot of people who suffer from indecision suffer from a feeling that they will be criticized if they make the wrong decision. Making wrong decisions is very good for you, as it allows you to reevaluate yourself, and once you are comfortable with screwing things up royally, you'll gradually avoid it. When you don't know, don't go. If you can't act powerfully, do nothing and wait for circumstances to change. And if they won't change or you can't change them, walk away.

I constantly feel as though people are playing games with me to their advantage. How do you avoid people manipulating you?

The first move is to avoid situations where people have power over you, and avoid as much as possible situations where you have emotional needs that others have to fulfill. That makes you vulnerable. The next thing is to learn to establish firm boundaries. You have to be able to look people in the eye and tell them when something is not acceptable. Let people know that they can't tread all over you. Of course, in certain circumstances, people do have power over you and therefore they can manipulate you. In this situation, the only way to escape manipulation is to move. However, if you have a simple life and you can move around fluidly, then there are not many forces that can really impinge upon you to any great extent.

I've been working on myself for a few years now, and I feel I've reached a point where I would like to share my insights with others and become a teacher. What's the best advice you could give to someone hoping to become a New Age lecturer/author?

The best advice to give someone wanting to become a New Age teacher is to go ahead, but be careful you don't lose your current financial support mechanism. What destroys most of the teachers is that they're desperate for book sales, customers, acknowledgment, and lectures. In that financial stretching and reaching, they disempower their message. If you have a powerful energy, you'll have a powerful message, and people will be drawn to you. But the important thing is you have to be financially self-sufficient, doing other things that earn you a living. Then you can start to teach, make tapes, and write books without worrying too much about whether they will be successful.

Remember, almost everything has already been said about a hundred times before, so you should try to bring some kind of originality to your teaching. That means going deep within yourself and pulling out a new idea, a new *modus operandi*, a new technology, a different format, something that hasn't been done before.

So, to really make any headway as a teacher, you need to be original, package your ideas cleverly and succinctly, and put them in easy-to-understand frameworks. Also, ideas and philosophies should be inexpensive if possible.

People are always saying trust your Higher Power or your inner guidance because it knows all the answers. I've tried to do this but have ended up worse off. Do our inner selves really hold all the answers, or is it better to just think things through logically?

You have to trust your intuition, your higher self, your sixth sense, and march on believing. However, it stands to reason that if a certain path is logical and obvious, then that's the way to go. Generally speaking, the rule of thumb is: If it feels right, it *is* right. If it doesn't feel right, it's not appropriate at that time. If a path has no particular energy, that usually means no in my book. In other words, I don't make a left turn unless I have a strong feeling that it is the way to go. If I'm ho-hum or ambivalent about a move, I wait and see if the energy builds or wanes, and then I act.

I have always been terrified by the thought of death. I do believe there is life after death, but something inside me is still so frightened of what will become of me when it eventually happens.

To reconcile a fear of death, you have to do battle with the ego, for it is your ego that fears death, not you. The ego is not only frightened of physical death, but any kind of death. That is why change is so hard for people—because they won't accept death. And what is change? Just the death of a previous pattern or relationship. The ego holds enormously to the patterns it understands, the ideas it understands, and it is absolutely adamant that no death should occur. To liberate yourself and become a true-blue warrior, you have to reconcile death. If you don't, you will constantly be a victim of it.

To overcome the ego's terrible death-fear, you have to make yourself accept death. A simple meditation is to hover above Earth in your mind's eye and visualize the planet with you not here. In other words, you are establishing a place of consciousness that is beyond your physical existence here. That really begins to confirm the idea that the planet will be here without your ego, personality, and physical body.

In *Whispering Winds of Change*, you say that truth is vital if you want to progress as a spiritual being. Can you explain why?

I think truth is vital because it is honorable to be truthful to yourself and other people, otherwise you're living a lie. In my book *Affirmations*, I talk a lot about variance. Variance is the discrepancy between the social image you project, and that which is true and real about your energy, your life, your financial status, and your relationships—in other words, the pretense of life. If your pretense of life—the image you have about yourself, or the ego's image of who and what you are—is vastly different from the truth, it creates an enormous amount of effort to sustain the illusion. We all know people who sustain the illusion of importance, or they sustain the illusion of being wise masters, or the illusion of being sexually desirable. All of that takes an enormous amount of effort. So truth is important because it allows you to relax.

In your tape series and book *Infinite Self: 33 Steps to Reclaiming Your Inner Power*, you discuss the courage of letting go in Step 3. When people tell you to "let go" of pain, anger, guilt, fear, and so on, exactly how do you do it? I've tried letting go in visualizations and meditations, but I find that I still haven't really let go in my everyday life. What practical things can I do from day to day to let go?

Letting go is a hard one. Every part of humanity is designed to hang on. We hang on to our family connections, to the certificate we got at school, to our money; we embrace and hang on to our children, we lock our car and hang on to it. I think the whole definition of letting go is to stand outside the emotion. I talk about it a lot in my books, especially in *Weight Loss for the Mind.*

Letting go by visualizing and meditating is tough, because you have to concentrate on the thing you're trying to let go of. So it's a bit self-defeating. I think it's important to understand that you are not the character who is going through the emotion.

A technique I used in my meditations was to visualize myself spinning away. First, I would see myself in my mind's eye, so I'd be looking at my face. I'd see myself doing "angry" because of, let's say, a business situation. Then I'd visualize myself spinning away from the angry energy, or away from the upset. That helped me create the feeling of being able to detach myself from it, observe that it wasn't me, and recognize that it was just a reaction I was going through.

All emotion is reaction to opinion. I talk about that a lot in my books. In order to feel any emotion, positive or negative, you have to first have an opinion. Usually the way to go past it all is to change the opinion. In other words, life isn't necessarily going to go the way you want it. It's not necessarily going to be in this way, on that day, at this time, in that format, and so on. The most important thing is to hang loose and go with the flow, bro'.

In *Miracles*, you discuss understanding one's life's mission. I honestly don't know what my life's mission is. Have you any suggestions on how I can find out?

Our mission in life breaks down into three things. First, we have to overcome fear and learn to love, not just ourselves but everybody—even those people that are fairly "arseholic." Next, we have to gather knowledge about ourselves, the world, people, the human condition, as well as the cosmos around us. Finally, we must serve others.

Any additional actions you take that assist you in becoming a more powerful transcendent being also form part of your life's mission.

Some people don't know who they are or what they want, and this is often because their life is too cluttered. In my books, I suggest that, if this is the case, you should start to eliminate things from your life—get back to the bare bones, so to speak. As you eliminate clutter, you will gradually feel more sure about what direction you want to take.

You've written a whole book on the power of silence. In this book, you talk about becoming an etheric being. You state that *knowing* you are an etheric being is different from *thinking* you *are* an etheric being. How can we tell the difference?

I've made the study of the etheric the main feature of my inner journey in this lifetime, and so I have gradually gained a modicum of knowledge about how it works. What we normally call feelings are in fact physical sensations. Even our emotions, which we sometimes refer to as feelings, are in fact outcroppings of our personality's opinions. When life enhances your opinions, you feel positive; and when life contradicts your opinions, you feel negative. Emotions are an outcropping of opinions and your reactions to circumstances.

I believe that true feelings exist only in the etheric, for the human body can only discern sensations. What we call feelings are not strictly feelings as such—they are reactions or sensations. I've had experiences where my etheric body is outside my physical body and distanced from it. When I tried to move an etheric limb and touch a wall, I'd feel the wall. However, that is not a sensation because it happens outside the body's mechanism. Similarly, if while in the etheric you experience an emotional reaction, such as seeing the love of the God Force, the emotion is expressed as a deep feeling. It rests somewhere in the very heart of your spiritual nature, and that feeling resonates throughout the etheric body—you are that feeling and it is you. The etheric is very sensitive, and the feelings you perceive from it are akin to all-knowing. It's a heightened state of awareness. You become the thing you are touching.

The way to go from *thinking* you are an etheric being to *knowing* you are an etheric being is to enter into a meditative state and visualize your subtle body moving around. Imagine it over on the other side of the room, for example. Once you feel you have mastered moving your energy around in trance, then try doing it in the waking state. The mental projection of the etheric can be done at any low brain speed, either in the waking state or in trance. So, for example, try relaxing yourself into a meditative state and try reaching for a person who is, say, walking on the other side of the street. Reach across mentally and, using your will, project your subtle body across the road and touch the person you are concentrating on. I call this "tapping." More often than not, they will look around, for they will feel your touch or your presence on their subtle body. Once you move the etheric around and use it, you'll know that you're an etheric being. It's not hard, I promise.

In your books, Stuart, you ask us how we know that our thoughts are ours. What do you mean by that, and if our thoughts aren't ours, whose are they?

We presume that our thoughts are ours because no one has ever challenged the idea. Modern technology can scan the brain and watch it working, but it can't scan thoughts. You can stimulate the brain and ask the patient what they are feeling or what reaction that stimulation caused, but you can't know exactly what a mind is thinking. Nor can you be certain that the electrical impulses you are observing are a result of that person's particular consciousness or some incoming thought from elsewhere.

I know this idea sounds bizarre and most neurologists would say it's crazy. I'm not saying the neurologists are wrong. It's just that they are looking at consciousness and the brain in an external, logical way rather than from a multidimensional view of mind and consciousness beyond the 3-D rotation, where thoughts flow back and forth instantly and automatically.

Now, this question would need 50 pages to really explain it properly, but here is the gist of it.

There is no space in consciousness, no distance. There are levels of perception layered by oscillation like strata of a cake, but it's all the same cake. Every bit of the global mind is technically able to be aware of every other bit, and how much you are aware of is limited by individual development. But it's all there. The consciousness we are normally aware of, the thing we call our "mind," is trained by, and a product of, its social situation — its location in the 3-D state. So ideas coming in from others don't seem strange because they are coming in from minds that are likewise programmed. So it's hard for an individual to realize that there are thoughts coming into their mind that are not their own.

If an incoming thought is totally out in left field, like it expresses a totally unknown idea or technology, then you might be able to say that it's not your own thought, for you would know that you didn't know those facts or that you weren't familiar with those ideas. But ideas that flood in are from ordinary people with the same ideas and motivations as yourself. So it's very hard sometimes to figure out what your ideas and impulses are, and what comes from other individuals or even from the collective mind of humankind.

It is natural to presume that the thoughts that come into your mind are automatically your thoughts. However, I believe we're all interconnected and that a fairly substantial percentage of your ideas—especially those that relate to people, places, and social situations outside your immediate life, or ideas of an inspirational nature—come into your mind from somewhere else.

Rupert Sheldrake talks a lot about morphic resonance. He maintains that we are all interconnected, so that when one person learns a task, it automatically becomes easier for other people to learn the same task. Evidence of this occurred after Roger Bannister managed to run a four-minute mile. For thousands of years, people tried to accomplish this feat, but as soon as Roger Bannister did it, a barrier was torn down and a dozen did exactly the same as Bannister shortly thereafter. Sheldrake says, for example, that through morphic resonance, people doing the crossword puzzle in the evening find it easier to do than the people who did it in the morning when the paper first came out, because there had already been an impact on that particular morphic field—the answers had been deduced by others.

What I've said in my books is, because one can project thoughts into people's minds and because one can move one's subtle body into the force field or physical body of another person, we cannot categorically say that all the thoughts we have are ours. In the extreme case of mass hysteria or collective hallucinations, for example, you can see how ideas jump so rapidly that instantaneously a group of people can act completely irrationally. Fear can also jump from one person to the next. If the person next to you is scared, it makes you feel uncomfortable and insecure. You can test this for yourself by getting on any airline flight that has a lot of first-time flyers, or vacationers who are not used to flying often. The fear you feel as you walk through the plane is intense, and it jumps back and forth between the passengers, affecting all of them. Yet in the coach section, it's more intense than, say, in first class, where there's usually a sense of tranquility. This is because there are fewer seats and they're spaced farther apart. The ease you feel in first class has nothing to do with the fact that they're going to serve you caviar and champagne once the aircraft takes off—it's all to do with the fact that there is less psychic pollution in first class.

In your tape series *Assertiveness*, you say, "I don't think there's an issue in the world worth defending. If you have to defend something, it means you don't believe it." I always thought that if you feel the need to defend something, it's not because *you* don't believe it, but because others don't?

The most important thing about defending yourself is that if you have to defend yourself virulently, it really means you're not very sure of yourself. If you really believe in something, you don't need to convince others. I think convincing others is a hopeless task because either people believe it or they don't. You can convince people simply by the energy of what you are. I don't think any intellectual waffling over issues does anything for you. I'm a great believer in not trying to convince people.

If you're a politician or a power freak, you might need to convince people so they will buy your stuff or buy your ideas or vote for your party. But someone on a spiritual path doesn't need to win over others. There is a sacredness in leaving the world alone and not disturbing things.

In *Miracles,* you talk about personal power and how to attain it. I tried the affirmation you suggested, but I feel there is more. Is there something else I can do to enhance my personal power?

Personal power comes from discipline and introspection, and it develops gradually over the years as you gain self-confidence. However, there are things you can do to enhance your power of visualization. In my book *The Quickening,* I talk about a system called "turbo-thought." You generate heat in the area of the root chakra—the kundalini—and from that sexual heat you bring a bubble of energy up to the heart chakra. Inside that bubble you place a vision of the thing or the conditions or the goal you're seeking. It has to be a symbol that represents the goal as a done deal, in its completed state. Now, in your mind's eye, hold the bubble of light in the area of your heart, visualize the symbol inserted into the bubble, then expel a short, sharp breath and allow the bubble of energy to explode throughout your system. This"turbo-thought" technique allows you to create, inside your subtle energy (the etheric), a holographic image of trillions upon trillions of molecules of etheric energy that depict the symbol of the vision or the goal you seek. You become a walking imprint of the thing or condition you desire. Your energy is now congruent with your goal, and so your probability field expands to its infinite potential.

You mention the "real you" in *The Secrets of Life*. I feel that my ego completely swamps the "real me," that part of myself that is pure, all-loving, and magnanimous. Is there anything I can do to make the real me stronger?

Because of our programming, we tend to think that our personality or intellect is the real us, so we will talk about "our possessions," "our life," "our feelings." It is only once you control the intellect, once you dominate your own mind, and once you control the negative influence of the programming you receive that you can begin to experience the infinite you. Discipline is the only way you can really perceive a higher dimension of self. It is through silence, introspection, and discipline that you come to an understanding of the infinite nature and the beauty of this evolution.

Try this: Breathe in, hold your breath momentarily, and imagine yourself expanding at an infinite velocity to the outer reaches of the universe. Then release your breath and see yourself coming back to your normal human shape and size. Repeat the process. In this way, you begin to become infinite within your finite human consciousness. It's a simple way of getting used to the idea. By concentrating on the infinite self, you finally become more infinite and less finite. It's just a matter of focus and, of course, a little bit of patience as you allow the process of change to consolidate in your life.

Why are we so afraid of changing the way we perceive ourselves? I know you write about the deceptive power of the ego in many of your books and it makes sense, but putting it into practice is different.

In the laws of the ego, you are not allowed to die. We spend millions making our ego feel special. In the laws of the ego, you cannot assail the ego's emotions. Our emotions are nothing more than an extension of the ego's opinions—nothing more. We elevate our emotions to a great scale. For the most part, our emotions are theatrical manifestations of the ego's opinions. For example, I want you to mow my lawn, you don't want to do it, and so I get aggressive or make threats. You get scared and mow the lawn. Simple. They are forms of manipulation. Even what we call romance is only an opinion of the ego. You have an opinion and you start cranking the emotion. So we live as prisoners of these opinions.

We establish these ideas such as "I have to be this . . . people have to see me in this way . . . things should be like that . . . ," and we create a legislation, a parliament. So our lives as individuals are exactly the same as our government. If you see your government as corrupt, if you see it as ineffectual, weak, full of itself, it is only a manifestation of the national mind-set. All of the democracies are the same. In fact, we don't even have democracies—all we have is a benign version of fascism. Why? Because a few fascist bastards control everything through secrecy, through manipulation of information, and obscuring the facts. You see them on television every night, and it is the wolf talking. But who talks for the chickens? We don't have anybody that talks for us. Have you ever heard anybody get up on television and say, "Let's get rid of this bunch of twits and scrub the systems?" It doesn't honor our people, it doesn't allow them to be free, it doesn't do anything for them. This perpetual injection of fear that you get is nonsense. Most humans die in their bed at a ripe old age—at least 90 percent in Western democracies. The idea that you are going to be raped and murdered and shot and killed by a bus is rubbish. There are very few people who need that experience.

I fly for a living, and every time I get on a plane that is empty, I feel incredibly safe because no empty planes crash. They just don't. They are always full when they go down. Why? Because there are millions of spirits who think, *I've had enough of this crap; I am out of here*. And their inner self says, *Here, try Flight 108 going to Timbuktu, that'll work. It will be terribly quick. You'll have a few moments where you are scared shitless, but then you'll be out of there.* The fact is, we are prisoners of our political egos, we are prisoners of these systems that are based on control. But here we are, fringe dwellers who feel different and who are different. We can't knock these systems down just yet, and we don't need to. The rebirth of Camelot, the rebirth of chivalry, the rebirth of goodness, the rebirth of fairness—real fairness, not emotional or political fairness, but real fairness based on energy —is coming.

But you'll have to be patient—and if you are an infinite being, you can be patient forever.

Chapter Three

WILDE ABOUT RELATIONSHIPS

What are your views on marriage and divorce?

Marriage was invented a long time ago as a contract between a heterosexual male and a heterosexual female. We can only trace romantic love back to about a thousand years ago. Prior to that, there wasn't any romantic love. It's an idea that has been invented, like a philosophy or a religion. It has been made very special.

In the olden days, when life expectancy was short and people lived 30 or 40 years at most, the idea of men and women being together for their whole lives was feasible, especially as they lived in the context of a sluggish energy that didn't change much. There wasn't a lot of difference between England in the 1400s and the 1700s, when it came to sexuality, marriage, relationships, and so on.

Sexuality burst open with the advent of the Pill and other birth control methods, and now relationships can move so much more quickly. Some marriages might last only 20 minutes, because everything has been said and done in that time. I think marriages, relationships, and energy get used up faster because our society is moving faster.

Also, somebody has to rethink how marriage works, because obviously the patriarchal system — where the male dominates and the female gives birth and stays in the home—is not appropriate for everyone anymore. Yet in tossing that idea out, we often have these archaic ideas that if the marriage doesn't work, the male is somehow supposed to sustain the female. So, on the one hand, we don't like the idea of the male dominating the female in the house, but once the male leaves, the law can say it's his responsibility to give the woman the home and sustain her. Of course, this creates a lot of problems because things are changing. We have to come to a middle ground where people think about what they actually want, or what is fair.

It's always seemed to me that romance is a money-making business. I used to say this in my seminars and receive howls of protest. Everybody likes to think that romance is a pristine, special thing and nobody is thinking of cash, security, prenuptial settlements, postnuptial divorce payments, and so on. I've always had the impression that in the USA, in spite of their modern way of thinking, when it comes to Saturday night and everybody's partying, there's a lot of horse trading going on. The guy who is rich and successful gets plenty of ladies, and the guy who doesn't have any money gets less. So there must be something about the economy of romance that seems to attract ladies up the higher end of the economic scale. Then again, you may possibly fall in love with a tramp if that's what you're supposed to do in this lifetime.

I don't think there will ever be a simple answer to marriage and divorce. Basically there is no point in hanging out with somebody you don't like. However, having said that, I do believe that there is a validity in staying together for the sake of children. So some people make a compromise. The rules of marriage are going to have to be rewritten. I'm not keen on the idea of single mothers, because I think children need the presence and influence of their father. I'm definitely not keen on the idea of single mothers raising kids with money from the government. So the whole thing is in a state of flux . . . we'll have to wait and see.

Whether you're heterosexual or gay, a sacred commitment is wonderful and can really increase your energy. It doesn't have to be a formal marriage, but by making that commitment, metaphysically you will bounce off your partner, and your partner will bounce off you, and bit by bit you can build each other up. You are reflected in your partner, and he or she is reflected in you, so you learn about yourself while simultaneously raising your energy. A solid, committed relationship is a wonderful thing and can create a lot of power. It can also be destructive and debilitating when it isn't going well. So it's a risky business.

What are your views on homosexuality?

I don't really have any views on homosexuality. I think people's sexual preferences are their own business. It's a good thing our society doesn't discriminate as much against gays and lesbians as it used to. It seems like society is gradually opening up. Certainly if you've ever been to Sydney, Australia during the time of the Mardi Gras, you'll know it's a real party. The homosexual community brings a lot of color and creativity to our society. There will always be homosexuals in our society, and it's important that we tolerate everybody. So it's all fine by me.

Do you believe in monogamy?

Yes, I think couples should be monogamous until such time as they don't want to be. It does help to create a sense of security, love, and commitment. However, I've said many times in my writings that we come together for growth, not for life. So if you can't get it together with your mate, then you have to keep moving.

Do you agree with abortion?

I do and I don't. I don't really believe it's right to kill a fetus, but then again, I don't believe it's right to tell a woman she has to have a baby. So I don't think there is ever a correct answer to this one. I'm sure women who have abortions have their reasons, but I can also see the other side of the argument.

When teenage children begin experimenting with alcohol and drugs, is it best to enforce a strict discipline on them from the outset, or let them learn their own lessons and avoid interfering with their evolution?

This is a difficult question to answer. I think it's important to enforce discipline upon children in relation to drugs and alcohol. However, teenagers are teenagers, and no amount of discipline will work if they don't want to listen. It's important to have them understand the destructive nature of drugs and alcohol, and somehow they either have to avoid them, or use them with caution. I think it's a matter of teaching children responsibility, and of course that will depend very much on the kind of family life they have experienced up to that point. So I don't think there is an all-encompassing answer to this one.

Do you think it's okay to raise children as vegetarians or vegans?

Yes, I think it's fine to raise children as vegetarians or vegans, just as long as they have a healthy, balanced diet.

I'm beginning to find my boyfriend annoying. As much as I love him, I can't stand the fact that he wants to spend every second of the day with me. I tell him I need space, but he takes it as an affront. How can I make him understand that I still love him even if I don't spend every spare minute of the day with him?

Tell your boyfriend not to take it personally, but you need some space. If he does take it personally, you have to explain to him that if he suffocates you to the point where you don't have any time for yourself, in the end the relationship will fall apart. I think it's important to send him off to do something he enjoys while you have some time to yourself.

My girlfriend wants to have an open relationship where both of us can have sex with others. She says she's doing it for "us," so we don't get bored. It's an appealing proposal, but I love my girlfriend and I don't want to jeopardize our relationship. What are your thoughts on open relationships?

I think relationships have to be open—in the sense that you must allow the other person to engage in the pastimes and pleasures they enjoy. Generally speaking, however, if your partner is involved in a sexual relationship with somebody else, while this may be exciting and erotic and interesting, eventually it will destroy your relationship. It's very difficult to maintain a perpetual relationship if both parties are not monogamous. In spite of a lot of modern ideas, the transfer of sexual energy back and forth between two people is a very important thing, and if it is not kept in a disciplined context, it will undermine the relationship. The idea of experimenting sexually with other people while trying to maintain a relationship usually doesn't work.

Both my relationship and my spiritual path are sacred to me, but it seems I must choose one over the other. Which is more important, a loving relationship with a partner who does not share my interest in spirituality, or a wonderful spiritual life without the partner of my dreams?

I think it's a terrible thing if you have to choose between your spirituality and your relationship. I certainly couldn't be in a relationship if my partner was antagonistic to my spiritual life and way of thinking. I think I *could* be in a relationship if they were neutral, though.

In modern relationships you often find that both parties might start out in a very Neanderthal tick-tock consciousness, then one party begins to work on themselves and really moves forward metaphysically and spiritually. This leaves the other Neanderthal member behind. Sometimes that will work fine, because a compromise takes place, and metaphysics and spirituality are simply not discussed. Then sometimes you can evolve yourself out of a relationship because you're moving quickly and your partner isn't.

If you've grown way beyond your partner, you might have to leave. I can't imagine a relationship that was so magnificent I'd want to give up my metaphysics or spirituality or my path toward God. Somebody else might think differently, but that's my view.

I have a burning desire to explore tantric sex, but my partner is not interested. What do you suggest?

This is a tough one. I think tantric sex manuals and books are laced with a lot of "ooh" and "aah" that doesn't amount to much. A lot of it is the raising of the kundalini from the root to the crown chakra, and I think you can do that quietly on your own. The heat of the sexual act creates energy, which you can mentally pull up the spine to the crown chakra. Visualizing it rising unblocks the etheric channel, and the power flows up the spine to the top of the head. You can create the effect of tantric sex without the other partner really knowing what's going on.

If you really want to explore tantric sex with a partner who is not willing, all I can suggest is that you ditch your partner and find another one. They're very interested in tantric sex in Germany. Whenever I've toured there, I've always had a lot of questions about tantra from the audience, and there are always a lot of tantra workshops happening. Go visit Germany.

How do you know when to persevere with a relationship and when to let go?

If you feel restricted or if you feel a tremendous amount of emotional pain, then you really need to see whether those knots and that restriction can be unraveled. If they can't, obviously it is the fault of the relationship and your reaction to the relationship, and you should probably let go. What is the level of restriction you feel? What is the level of emotional pain you feel? Are you getting out of this relationship as much as you're putting in? If there is an overdraft, an imbalance in the emotional-energy bank account, then you need to reassess the relationship.

It seems weird that people nowadays are so scared of being on their own. Being on your own somehow seems like a failure. When you think about it, being on your own actually exhibits maturity. Most people who think they need someone in order to feel safe and secure probably don't need anybody at all. In fact, they probably ought to live on their own for a bit and become self-sufficient.

My 13-year-old daughter is displaying a great interest in meditation and metaphysical ideas, such as astral traveling and mediumship. I'm worried that she might be too young, and wonder when is the right age to encourage children to learn more about these concepts.

I don't think there is any problem with children experimenting with meditation, astral travel, and so on. Generally speaking, kids take it all in stride, and I wouldn't worry at all. I would even encourage them to learn about some of these ideas, disciplines, and concepts. It certainly won't be at the forefront of their attention, because other things will be more important at that age. But it may stand them in good stead at a later date. I don't think there's anything to worry about.

My child is almost school age, and I'm trying to decide whether to send him to a government school, an alternative Steiner-type school, a private boarding school, or educate him at home. Each seems to have its advantages and disadvantages. What do you suggest?

I'm not an expert on education; however, many government schools suffer from a lack of facilities, and they can't afford to hire top people. Also, because the children are taken from all walks of life, some are an energy drain and disruptive. I would certainly not send my child to a government school if I was financially able to send him elsewhere.

I sent my little boy to a Steiner-type school [a school reflecting the philosophy of Austrian metaphysician Rudolf Steiner], and he did very well there. It's a matter of what one can afford, but I'm not a great believer in the government system, so I would always try to look for something alternative. I do know of children who have been educated entirely at home, but they didn't turn out too good, in my view. They seemed somewhat disjointed and unable to cope, and they seemed to lack pals their own age. But for some people who travel a lot, for example, they might have no choice but to educate their children at home.

I would like to raise my children outside the tick-tock mentality, but fear they will have problems adjusting if they are confronted with it later on. How can I achieve a balance between the two?

I wouldn't worry too much about trying to raise children outside the tick-tock mentality, because, in many ways, the only way past tick-tock is *through* it. If you send a child into a school system that is a bit "tickety-tock," or they go to a university or join the military, it's okay because everybody needs a bit of that in order to transcend it. I would teach the child about the infinity within; about serenity; expose them to the writings of some of the great mystics such as Lao-Tzu, Buddha, and so on; and allow them to come to their own freedom. It doesn't matter if people experience a bit of tick-tock, because, in the end, they're going to see it for what it is. The other thing is that no matter how far you go away from tick-tock in your feelings or your mind, you always have to do business with it in the end and encounter it as you go along.

In *The Secrets of Life,* you say, "Love is not an emotion." Are you referring here to unconditional love?

Love is not an emotion in a spiritual sense because the love of God is an intrinsic quality that flows through the God Force and all things. As I've often said, human emotions are based on opinions, so the love you have for another individual will be based somewhat on the opinions you have of them: that they're a caring person, or a nice person, or they're good to you, and so forth. The love of the God Force is real love because it is the intrinsic quality of that electromagnetic energy—it is an all-encompassing inclusiveness unbounded by definition.

In your book *Affirmations,* you talk about learning to detach from acceptance. I find I'm constantly searching for acceptance from others. I realize this is probably because I don't accept myself. Have you any suggestions on how I can cultivate more self-acceptance and stop putting myself down so much?

The need for acceptance from others is a natural human tendency. However, the basis of it comes from insecurity. It stems from the way we interacted with our family members, siblings, and friends as a young person.

As we grow up through our teenage years, we find the need to join the society of our friends, and—in order to join the society and feel solid as a personality—we program ourselves into needing people's acceptance. Accepting yourself is an act of spiritual empowerment because it allows you to understand that you didn't come here to be perfect. You can absolve yourself of your deficiencies and promise to try harder in the future, and you can accept your successes and your strengths.

In that humility and spirituality, you understand that you have a perfection that exists in the light of God; you are potentially an angel inside a physical body. Security comes from feeling connected to all things. It is beyond the intellect, the personality, and the mind. It's an inner sense of knowing, which only comes once you've managed to control the mind.

So, once you see yourself from an infinite perspective and don't need to win people's acceptance, you can be kinder and more gentle toward yourself. You can understand that you're in a state of imperfection—that you're here on this Earth plane to learn from it, and to gradually improve, strengthen, and return back to the light where you and I and all of us belong.

In *The Force,* you say that it's "impossible to say that what others are going through is either good or bad: it is neither." A lot of my friends complain about how "bad" they've had it. True, most of them have had difficult lives, but I'm sick of hearing it. Do you have any suggestions about what I could say to my friends so they can get on with living life rather than complaining about it?

I don't think you can say to somebody who feels bad: "Don't feel bad." The most you can do is try to take people away from the reactions of their ego/personality and get them to see outside of themselves. The ego/personality is myopic in that it usually looks only at itself; it's not particularly aware of a greater evolution beyond itself. If you can carry people away from themselves to a global or galactic vision, or even if you just show them the beauty of nature, it helps them to go beyond the various opinions that are making them feel unwell.

In *Silent Power*, you write, "Trying to win people over and hoping the world will accept you for your wonderfulness is futile and weak." I find I have to do this every day in the business world. I work in advertising and find that my career is all about trying to impress others. It certainly becomes tiresome, but how can I avoid it?

Trying to win people over in business—where you're trying to sell them a story, a commercial idea, or a product—is completely different from trying to win acceptance by accommodating people in your private life. Naturally, if you're working in advertising, you have to make the right noises and rub people's egos the right way in order to be successful. However, whether in business or in your private life, the secret is to impose firm boundaries. It's a matter of saying: "When you do this, I will react like that," or "This kind of action is not acceptable to me." You have to let people know what you will accept and what you won't accept without any rancor. With good boundaries, you don't need to win people over, and you can always keep people from violating your space. You can have an individual identity and an individual set of rules, and as long as you can explain this to people equitably and kindly, they can either abide by the rules or they can walk away. Or, alternatively, you can walk away.

You talk about "silent communication" in your books. What exactly do you mean by that?

I have come to believe, through watching the etheric state, that we are all in silent subliminal dialogue with each other. I've observed the flashes of energy that pass back and forth between people, and I've seen people react to thoughts that are projected toward them. Thoughts jump. How many times have you been thinking about something obscure and the person next to you mentions the very same thing?

Silent communication generally comes about when you are thinking in the direction of another person, rather than concentrating inwardly toward your own thoughts and feelings. Silent communication can be in the form of prayers uttered silently toward people, or silent affirmations. Then there is actual dialogue that is spoken mentally in the direction of another person. It is telepathic transfer of energy, and hopefully it is silent dialogue that offers love or encouragement of some sort.

Also, in the etheric state, you have the ability to step into the subtle energy of another person. For example, in my *Developing the Sixth Sense* tape series, I talk about moving the etheric—the subtle body—out of your physical body, turning your subtle body to face you, and then stepping backwards with your etheric into the physical body of a person you're talking to. Visiting another person etherically in this way is okay, providing you're not manipulating them or making them do things they don't want to do. It's a way of being with them, concentrating on that person. In the end, concentration is a form of love; when you're focusing upon a person, you are in the act of loving them.

Try this: Start projecting love to people as you pass them in the street. The idea is to imagine (generate) a deep and resonating sense of love in your heart and expel a short breath, firing the love in another person's direction—try to hit them in the heart with your love missile. Pick total strangers. Velocity is the key. Breathe out a short sharp breath and use the force of your will, and whack 'em hard in the heart with all the love you can muster.

And as you touch them etherically with your fast-moving dollop of love, notice them blink or move their eyes suddenly. Sometimes you'll see them turn around like they're looking for where the energy came from, but they don't understand what it is they are feeling. Often you'll see them smile, and sometimes they'll start talking to themselves. It's a fun game, but it tires you out after a while so don't overdo it.

Health warning: If you manipulate or project evil, or you use your powers to the detriment of others, you create a lot of bad karma. Gradually those evil thoughts and projections move from their initial evil state, and they begin to solidify on the astral plane. They take on a phantasmagorical form that comes alive and gradually develops a mind of its own. It needs energy to sustain itself, and the first available source of energy is your life force, so the phantom you have created by your thoughts starts to suck on you, making you sick, tired, and listless. Eventually it can kill you. You get eaten by your own monster.

In your tape series *Loving Relationships*, you explain how females have a natural spiritual balance. You also mention that when women figure that out and stop trying to compete with male energies, they will begin to know their power. Do you have any thoughts on how they might be able to do this in a balanced way? It seems like the role models we see of women who have "made it" today are women who have done so by pushing their way through.

It's true that we seem to see the role models who take a more "yang," pushy attitude to life.

However, you have to qualify what you mean by "making it." In the ego's currency, "making it" is money, glamour, success, power, fast cars, and the like. In my view, making it is more of a spiritual exercise, so there are millions upon millions of women who have made it quietly in a spiritual way who would not be considered successful in the ego's world.

If you adopt the ego's currency for your life, then you do have to push. We live in a patriarchal society that requires yang types of action, investment, shoving, self-promotion, advertising, and so on. If you work in the currency of the higher self or the infinite self, then making it is something very different.

Obviously, one needs to develop a balance—a certain amount of "making it" in order to be creatively and financially successful, and a certain amount of embracing one's feminine spirituality. I know loads of soft, feminine ladies who are self-made millionaires, so it can be done. Women have to walk a fine line between making a living and asserting themselves so they're not used and manipulated by other people. But then again, the balance is the same for males, because the tendency for males is to push so hard and to strive with such zeal that they push the very thing they want away from themselves. Many males tend to overwork themselves and lose track of their childlike qualities and their inner yin softness.

I've been in a number of unhealthy relationships that have left me drained and fragile. I hang on to the belief that my soulmate is out there somewhere. Am I living in a fantasy? Is there really such a thing as a soulmate?

There are definitely soulmates, and it's very possible that you may find somebody with whom you are compatible. However, many people who are raising their energy and working on themselves find it very difficult to sustain "old style" relationships. The patriarchal systems on which they are based are too restrictive; they are often designed to impose obligations and authority over the parties involved.

Nowadays, people who are spiritually aware and evolving need a lot of space, and it is often difficult to find another person who is secure enough to allow you to have that space. I've always recommended that you marry yourself first. I know people who have gone through formal ceremonies with themselves in the bathroom mirror. Marry yourself first, be content, be secure. Then if you can find a compatible person who is also solid and content with themselves, you have the makings of a pair of perfect soulmates.

Humans are very complex, and because we all have so many emotions to deal with and issues to work through, successful relationships also depend on a formal system of communication—not just a chat in the mornings and evenings when you've got a minute—a system whereby you spend an hour or two together on a regular basis at an appointed time, where you share your feelings, and express any concerns that have come up, without making your partner wrong. Your partner, in turn, can express their concerns, and together you can work on how things can be sustained at a high level of energy.

It's also important to remember that, nowadays, the energy of many people is oscillating so quickly, and there are so many "custodians of light" that the relationships you have can be very meaningful and yet short. Because of the speed both of you are oscillating at, you can complete everything there is to complete in the relationship and move beyond each other quite quickly. My old teacher used to say that you come together for growth, not necessarily for life. If your relationship lasts all your life, well, that's a beautiful thing. But, of course, nowadays every relationship has to accommodate enormous amounts of change, because society is changing rapidly and we live in "high-energy" times.

Chapter Four

WILDE ABOUT ABUNDANCE

What is the most important thing we should teach our children about money?

That there is lots of it, and it's easily available.

What were you taught about money?

My mother was a university professor and received a normal teacher's salary. My father was a naval officer and then a diplomat who also received a regular salary. So, I suppose what I was taught about money was that it comes in small, regular packets. However, I soon untaught myself that and headed off to fairer pastures.

I've worked a lot on my abundance consciousness over the years, but I've never really succeeded in getting past money worries and making ends meet day to day. What's the best thing I can do to heighten my money-making abilities?

There are only three things people buy: knowledge, a service, or a product. No matter how much you work on your abundance consciousness, and no matter how open and loving you become, in the end you have to have something of value to sell to others. The trick to abundance is finding something to sell—something people really need, that helps them raise their energy, perhaps makes their life easier; or that feeds their ego in some way by making them smarter, prettier, or more important.

Look for something people will buy. If you can, try to find something you don't have to deliver to people personally on a day-to-day basis, hands on. Knowledge is easy to sell because it can be produced in books, tapes, CD-ROMs, and so forth. Products are easy to sell because you can buy and sell them. Services are usually performed personally, so unless you charge a hell of a lot of money, offering people a service can sometimes become a rather low-paid prison. But it may be the starting point whereby, through giving your services, you develop other ideas, products, and knowledge you can sell to others. Look for what you're going to sell—that's the key to abundance.

If people ask you for money, should you give it to them, and why?

In my book *The Force,* I suggest giving people the things they ask for. However, I've found myself getting into a lot of trouble with this over the years because I didn't mean you had to give your whole life away. What I meant was, if somebody asks to borrow the lawnmower, lend it to them. In other words, don't be a tightass—be open, loving, and free, and share your abundance.

When people ask you for money, what they're really asking for is energy, and they shouldn't do it because we're each responsible for generating our own energy. I must say I don't like lending people money. I've found that when you do so, eight times out of ten that's the last you see of them and the money. What you have to do is either say no or just *give* them the money. Then there is no energy around who owes whom.

Generally speaking, I think it's good to be open and to share. However, if somebody comes along and they want your trousers, you don't have to take them off and walk around in your underwear. There is a natural balance between being generous and not allowing people to use you.

If you are a generous person and allow your money to flow, is it then okay to ask other people for money if you hit a rough patch?

Yes, I don't think it is a problem asking people for money if you hit a rough patch. The important thing is you're not going to make other people responsible for your energy.

One of the big problems in Western societies is that somehow people are becoming convinced that somebody else owes them a living, medical care, and welfare—"I'm a single mother, I'm entitled to a free home and money," "I'm a divorced father," "I'm unemployed." Of course, metaphysically speaking, that isn't correct. There is definitely a place for charity and kindness, but the idea that you can just underwrite someone's energy forever is absolute rubbish metaphysically, and it creates a warped, somewhat sick society.

I lay the blame for the disease of our societies partly on television and partly on the idea that, because you are a citizen, you are automatically owed enough energy to sustain yourself. When there is no call for you to sustain the energy yourself, the ego kicks back and becomes self-indulgent and lazy. Our societies suffer enormously from the projections of these characteristics.

Asking for money is fine if you need to, as long as you give it back when you're in the flow and don't make a habit of it. In the end, you have to believe in yourself and create your own energy.

It seems to me that you are against the welfare state, but surely we need a system that provides for the weaker members of society.

We do need a system that provides for people, but we don't need the current system. Debt is one of the mechanisms used by big business and government to control ordinary people. Welfare is a form of debt. Let me explain. When a recipient gets his or her benefit check, they don't have to pay the money back, so they are under the illusion that they don't owe anyone. But in reality they have incurred a debt on an energy level; they've gotten something for nothing.

The entire universe is designed around some very simple laws relating to energy and how it is generated, conserved, or used. Some say God designed those laws; others say it had to be that way in order for this universe to exist. Whatever your view, the laws that govern energy are natural and symmetric, and they are equally applicable on our planet as they are in a galaxy two billion light years away.

Now, you can use emotion, ego, politics, big business, power, greed, and control trips to temporarily bend those universal rules, but in the end, the natural law is bigger than the manipulators and their ability to bend circumstances. The first law of thermodynamics underwrites the whole universe, and it requires the conservation of energy, or more precisely, the sum of mass and energy is conserved. In other words there is no "free lunch" in the natural law. The government borrows money to sustain the welfare state, and in the end there will be an implosion of energy to correct the imbalance.

The sort of welfare state we need is one that assists the weak and helpless, and empowers the able-bodied. If every able-bodied person that receives money from the government was suddenly cut off, the taxpayers could easily afford and sustain those that are really in need. Over the years, however, the system has encouraged everyone to expect payment for simply existing.

The natural laws will not allow this state to exist forever. An electron can borrow energy for a split second to move to a higher orbit, but an instant later it has to pay it back and return (decay) to its natural state—the state that it can sustain with its own natural energy. Our societies will have to make the correction, for we are allowing the ego to let us oscillate at a higher level on borrowed energy. The current system based on ego, politics, and illusion is, in fact, unnatural, and it will have to adjust or mayhem will ensue.

If someone in a store undercharges you without realizing it, is it best to own up, or thank the universe for delivering more abundance?

If someone undercharges you and you notice it, pay them the right amount, especially if you agreed upon the price. If the assistant gives you more change than you're entitled to and you notice it, then it's only honorable and decent to give that money back. I think it's very important to be honorable, correct, and honest in your dealings with people. Then again, if you're walking down the street and find $1,000 on the ground and it doesn't belong to anybody in particular, then it's yours.

In the eyes of the universe, is it dishonorable not to pay back money you owe?

In the universality of Spirit, there is no high or low, good or bad, honest or dishonest. However, in one's own personal morality, there has to be. So, if you borrow money from people, you are entitled to pay it back, especially if you have consumed it personally. If you lose money that you borrowed for a business venture and all parties agreed to the risk, then you don't have to pay it back. If you borrow $5,000 from a group of people who are offering capital to start a fruit store and the store falters, well, that's just a commercial risk. It depends on the terms and conditions under which you have taken the money in the first place.

Do you think there will ever come a time when world economies collapse and paper money is worthless?

Yes, definitely. In fact, it's actually happening as we speak, because the paper money of the major trading nations is decreasing in value with every year that passes. The total amount of government debt is rising, with America leading the way. So, there will be a time when paper tender will become worthless and a new paper currency will be created. Of course, at that point you will need to be in gold or assets if you don't want to lose everything.

What do you feel are the most sound investments to make in the coming years?

I've become very confused as to what a sound investment is. I've been watching the stock markets climb into the stratosphere and beyond any expectations that I had. I'm not keen on stocks and shares anymore because, although they keep rising, they have to fall eventually. I think sound investments will be small real estate holdings with a few acres of land in rural areas that are nice and safe and a long way from urban cities. That's my idea of a sound investment. In the past I've never been keen on real estate, but I've changed my mind now.

Chapter Five

WILDE ABOUT POLITICS

WILDE ABOUT POLITICS

Do you believe there is such a thing as freedom?

Freedom is relative—the further you move away from your relatives, the more freedom you have! Seriously, though, there are varying degrees of freedom. As you move up through the mineral, vegetable, and animal kingdoms, the more freedom of movement a collection of molecules has, and the greater the power and complexity of their evolution. So freedom is defined by the parameters of movement an organism enjoys. It's also, in the metaphysical sense, the power of the oscillation of energy—the velocity, if you like. In human terms, it's also the power to influence others with one's energy. In its simplest terms, freedom is defined by the extent of your choices.

Within humanity, degrees of freedom vary. There are people who are very rich and technically free, but they are imprisoned by their greed or fears, often tangled in endless squabbles over money. Others may be almost penniless but truly free, for they have the mobility to wander the land, consuming very little and needing little to sustain themselves emotionally and physically. They are simple and complete. The name of the game is, get rid of most of your self-imposed personal rules and restrictions, then try as best you can to work around most of the rules of tick-tock.

Do you think the democratic system allows space for the individual?

The modern democratic system definitely does not allow enough space for the individual. We need a society that is ordered, lawful, and cares for its weaker members. But we also need a society where people are free to operate without the intrusion, surveillance, and permission of those people who govern the country.

What we need is a democratic system whereby the voters appoint administrators who have the voters' wants and needs at heart. In other words, we need governments that are employed by the citizens, not governments that rule over the citizens. The democratic system will fragment and eventually collapse within a generation or two, and it will have to be replaced by smaller, more manageable units of government.

What are your beliefs on censorship?

Basically, I don't think there should be any censorship. I think people ought to have the right to say what they want. However, I do understand that to live in a society, we do need certain moral boundaries. Two people in the privacy of their own home can get up to whatever they both agree on, but the media has to have a little decorum and not infringe on other people's privacy by broadcasting or publishing socially offensive stories.

It seems to me that in the USA, censorship is fairly extreme. People are scared to contradict anyone else. A lot of American thought is being straight-jacketed into a slightly left-of-center political correctness that doesn't allow for anybody to stand up and say, "Excuse me, this is a bunch of rubbish. Why don't we change things?" So it does seem to me that there is a censorship imposed because people are scared of negative reactions, scared of losing readers or viewers, and therefore advertising dollars.

On the other hand, Australia seems to be overrun with opinions but lacks wise direction. Australia doesn't need censorship, but perhaps it does need more informed debate.

I read in one of your books that you can't divorce politics from spirituality. Can you explain this, Stuart?

The main part of our spirituality is to learn to love in a world that is intrinsically restricted and dominated by ego and fear. We have to express our spiritual journey in the context of a physical body that exists in a society, so it's impossible to divorce politics from spirituality when politics impinges so dramatically on one's freedom.

For example, a political system that is in cahoots with bankers and the multinationals will seek to write rules that sustain such an elitist association. The government is above the law, and the multinationals are beyond the law for they can take their business anywhere. So, although they have to abide by the rules theoretically, they exercise enormous power. They are the employers of the ordinary people, so it's not hard for them to get the government to write rules that serve the corporate purpose.

All this regulation and appeasing of the bankers imposes restriction upon people. The idea is to create societies of drones who will give their lives to the institutions and support the government, while the government spends money like a drunken gambler. A system that controls wages and the conditions of labor—while taxing people 55 percent or more of their income—in effect controls people's ability to express themselves, while simultaneously capturing or controlling 55 percent of their mobility.

We come to the Earth plane to purchase experiences, to collect knowledge, and to understand ourselves in the context of creativity and action. Purchasing action and experiences is part of our spiritual journey as humans. And in a political situation, where mobility is restricted and commercial activity is regulated in favor of big business, where most of the proceeds of your efforts are taken from you, it naturally reduces your ability to experience life, to learn, and grow. So one can't divorce politics from spirituality.

Unfortunately, our leaders are 35 to 40 years behind the main thrust of consciousness. The driving forces in politics are globalization, monetary policies designed by bankers, domination by big business, surreptitious international standardization and regulation, multiculturalism, one-world government, the cashless society, and endless debt to sustain the system. The idea is to homogenize our societies, to lose or disempower the individual, to marginalize dissent via control, to manipulate the media, and to build societies of drones that will work for low wages and suffer punitive taxes to sustain the elitist order.

Yet, the mind-set of ordinary people is going the other way. They are becoming more conscious;

they want to be individuals and express themselves. They have woken up to the idea that debt is a form of imprisonment. They want mobility and quality of life.

Tax was sold to people in a socialist guise, but people are waking to the reality of the old manipulation, which said that paying half or more of your money to the government was reasonable, for you were helping your fellow citizens. Of course we have come to see this for the lie it is, for much of the money never reaches the citizens. And what does reach the citizens makes them dependent on the system. It disempowers people, truncating their creativity and forward movement.

As the consciousness movement has grown, people have moved away from the manufactured mind-set of consent, and toward liberty and freedom and the empowerment of individuals and small groups of people. The hippie ashram of the 1960s was the forerunner of our society's future, where small groups work together to become self-sufficient; where society, love and friendship, leisure and time off, creativity, and care for the environment are more important than the nine-to-five imprisonment of tick-tock, which only offers the *illusion* of security, not actual security. Security comes from local society, friendships, connections, the love of people and God, and a respect for the natural ebb and flow of nature.

Security stems from well-being and a debt-free, stress-free existence.

So, the minds of the conscious people are going one way, and the government and the institutions are going the other way. The revolutions and upheavals that were a part of the collapse of communism will become common in our Western nations as people come to realize that they are victims of a huge con game. The days of the big families, the bankers, and the sleazy political collusion that sustains the great lie are numbered. Spirituality is moving to a new level; it's a natural part of human progress, and politics is moving the other way. Politics will lose, and spirituality will win in the end.

Have you ever considered getting into politics?

Yes, I have, because sometimes when you watch the politicians on television, they're so crooked and phony. It would be magnificent if we could have a system that was at least straight, and not built on power and ego. So I think it would be terrific fun to be president for just a few months. But when I think of dealing with the mechanism of politics, the bureaucracy, a world that involves mind-numbing jostling for power, importance, and specialness, and the back-biting that goes on, I think politics would definitely, absolutely, and categorically make me throw up.

In your book *Whispering Winds of Change*, you devote a chapter to exposing the lies we are fed by the government, media, and other powerful groups. Do you suggest staying abreast of current affairs in order to detect the lies, or is ignorance a better option?

Staying abreast of current affairs is important. However, you need to do it very minimally. I suggest you buy papers and magazines rather than watching television because a lot of television media coverage is laced with tick-tock emotion, or is slanted toward favoring one particular view or another. The newspapers can often get pretty warped as well, but magazines devoted to current issues with a straightforward, investigative agenda can give you a clearer view of things with more journalistic integrity and less bias to sensationalism.

But the media will rarely use anything that contradicts the status quo, or the accepted norm. If you've ever seen the *New York Times,* the front page says, "All the news that is fit to print." Of course that pretty much sums it up. They will print what fits the reader, so you never get any contradictions.

It is important to stay somewhat distanced from current affairs, because our poor little planet is getting sicker and sicker. I must say that sometimes, if I watch the news a few nights in a row, I begin to despair. I don't think ignorance is better than knowledge. I think that what you have to do is to somehow stay current with what's going on in the world without getting sucked in. Use the Internet, as it's full of real, uncensored information.

Society is made up of a mountain of rules and regulations. Why do you think this is?

Society's rules and regulations are supposed to foster conformity. The idea is that, the more rules you have, the less things can go wrong and the safer people will feel. Up to a point, rules serve a purpose in defining reasonable behavior. However, nowadays, the plethora of rules is just part of the power trip the governing elite imposes upon the people from above. The more you can create yourself as an elite Godlike figure who has power over the people, the more you establish the phony idea of immortality within your ego. So in many ways, the rules and regulations imposed on us are really the product of the bureaucrats' desire for immortality. By having power to control, manipulate, fine, tax, imprison, and regulate people, they establish themselves as Godlike and therefore distant from the fate of humans, which is to die.

The bureaucrats know that the system is melting underneath them. However, their quest for immortality is driving them to tighten the rules and regulations, in the hope that the system that serves them so well will be perpetuated. Nothing will sustain the current system indefinitely, for it is built and sustained on a mountain of debt. The power exercised by governments is illusory. Unfortunately, for the next ten years or so, we will see an ever-increasing level of government surveillance and harassment. It's the nastier side of the world ego trying to dominate ordinary people who are becoming more free in their consciousness.

Chapter Six

WILDE ABOUT THE ENVIRONMENT

What do you see as the role of our governments in relation to environmental issues such as global warming, deforestation, waste management, and pollution?

In the late 1980s and early 1990s a lot of left-wingers got into the environmental movement, using it to crank their politics. A lot of that global-warming rhetoric and so on was hyped out of all proportion. However, I think it's very important that our governments control waste management and pollution. In particular, it's important to protect the water supply. Most of the planet's water supply is tremendously polluted. If you filter water, you can see how much crud it contains. This is the water our government tells us is pure. The crud you can see is quite frightening, and who knows how much is in there that you can't see?

With the population increasing, it's going to get more difficult to tackle these ecological/environmental issues. The spirit of humanity must feel threatened because we're creating more humans. This is especially so in developing countries, where basic survival is such a tough game that environmental concerns are less imperative.

But the planet exists in a state of balance. I'm a great believer in the Gaia theory, the planetary balance. Everything will get sorted out in the end. That's the way God planned it and, thankfully, the government cannot change that.

How important and/or effective do you think environmental groups such as Greenpeace, Friends of the Earth, and the Conservation Foundation are?

The various ecological groups have made a major impact on the world and our attitudes toward the planet. Some of those characters are really courageous, although I've met a few virulent environmentalists I wasn't keen on because they were so angry. But, taken as a whole, these various groups make us aware of important environmental and ecological issues and provide a collective opportunity for us to get involved if we wish.

Do you have a strong connection with nature? Where is your favorite place in nature?

Yes, I do have a strong connection with nature on a deep inner level. A lot of my life I've had to live in cities, but I was never comfortable there. My favorite place is in the mountains. I like the mountains of New Mexico. They're high and dry, and there is a mysticism there, a strangeness, a power. I've never been keen on beaches, but there are others who absolutely adore the water. I think I must have drowned in a previous incarnation, because the idea of bobbing at sea on a boat bothers me a lot. In fact, I rarely go out in boats, and I don't even like swimming in the sea. But I love nature, and I believe it's the building block of our spirituality.

The cruelty that is inflicted upon animals upsets me. What do you think about the evolution of animals?

I believe that animals belong to a group soul, so each species is actually one metaphysical atom that encompasses the collective soul of that animal. Species come and go over periods of millions of years, in the same way that humans come and go over a period of 70 years. I believe that, as a species evolves, it creates a spiritual identity, and that identity, in my view, is eternal.

When a person takes an animal out of its natural habitat and away from its species, and loves and cares for the animal like a family pet, then that animal leaves the collective evolution of its animal group soul and takes on an individualized evolution. When that animal dies, I believe it evolves inside the evolution of the human who loved it and gave it the most care.

The cruelty inflicted upon animals is very sad, but you have to remember that our world, with all its technology and sophistication, is still barbaric for the most part. You only have to go into our urban neighborhoods to see the barbaric way "sophisticated" humans treat each other. Most of our population lives in developing countries where respect for human life is often minimal. You can see that we haven't even mastered respect and kindness for our own species, let alone the animal species.

If one animal perishes as an act of cruelty or barbarism, the group soul of that animal still exists. Even when the last of the species dies, the group continues to evolve. It is as eternal as you are.

In the finite sense, our cruelty to animals is an externalization of our barbarism, egoism, and self-centeredness. But there is an infinite perspective that says that animals are as immortal as we are.

Gradually, over time, we'll become more respectful and kind to each other and to the animal kingdom.

What do you think of animal testing?

I'm 100 percent against it, except in rare cases of important medical research. The cruelty we inflict on animals really pains me, and the idea of testing cosmetics on rabbits and other animals is incredibly unfair and really bad karma. I applaud companies that highlight how cruel animal testing is. By taking a stand against this barbaric practice, they force other manufacturers to follow.

The anti-fur movement is similar. Once people started making their anti-fur-coat statements, it completely destroyed the industry. I notice now that fur coats are again coming back into fashion, but in the long run, wearing a fur coat is a no-no. I believe that in a generation or two, coats made from killing animals will be an extinct trade.

Do you think the dolphins and the whales know anything we don't? Do you believe in the healing power of dolphins?

I'm not sure about the dolphins and whales. They're obviously very intelligent beings, and they have their own communication system. They say dolphins make 30,000 different sounds. Any species that has such a complicated communication system must know things we don't know, because they communicate in a language we don't understand.

However, I'm not sure about the idea that dolphins hold some great spiritual message for the planet. If people believe in dolphins, in the sanctity of the animal kingdom, the water kingdom, then that's a wonderful thing. I suppose what the dolphin teaches us is compassion, caring, and kindness for the animals—which is very different from the wanton, mindless consumption and destruction that is so much a part of our society today. So anything that helps increase our consciousness is all well and good.

How can we stop the planet from destruction? When I read the papers or hear the news, I get the feeling that there isn't much we can do to save it. Our natural resources are being usurped and polluted, and people are starving. Is it too late?

The idea that this planet is lacking in things is a concept for the brain-dead. We've got more than we can ever cope with. The idea that it is all falling apart is true. The ego's world is falling apart; the ego's opinion, the world ego, our national egos are all falling apart. But our planet isn't.

Our planet is fine. Yes, we have to care for it and look after it, but it isn't about to collapse.

Every generation of people that has been on this planet has thought this was the end, because the ego cannot reconcile its own end. If it is conking out, then everything else must be conking out, too. It's that apocalyptic "end-of-the-world" idea that the ego has. It thinks, *Hey, if I'm dying, everyone else has to die, too. I can't be the only twit who has conked out while everybody else is having a nice time.* You can see it for what it is—nothing more than your opinions.

Get away from your opinions, don't worry about it when things contradict you, don't worry about it when you hear things you don't like, and don't worry about how it is supposed to be. Just stay focused on who you are and what you want. If you keep moving, suddenly this etheric inside of you will start to grow very quickly because you will be liberated.

Chapter Seven

WILDE ABOUT THE WORLD

In the past few years, I have met and spoken with many people in the world who are not satisfied with the status quo. I would even go as far as saying that the majority of people I know are what you call fringe dwellers. But if there are so many of us on the planet, how come not a lot is changing? It seems that, if anything, the world is becoming a more dangerous and frantic place to be.

You have to understand that fringe dwellers are a minute part of the world. We don't amount to even one percent of this planet yet. But the message is going out, and I believe we are all in silent communication with each other.

What's happening is that, while there are millions of us who have adopted this fringe-dweller mentality, the system wasn't designed for this type of being. Our people are only as good as what they create. That is why societies that are not based on honoring the creators will eventually collapse. You only have to look at our own societies. If you are a creator, you will be extremely discriminated against, because our systems regard creators as not being of any value to them. The figureheads running these systems just want to buy votes, and they need your energy to sustain the political manipulation. So, if you open a business or invent something, five minutes later you will have the bureaucracy trying to figure out how to regulate the hell out of you and take your money to keep themselves in power. There is no system in this world that you can get rid of on your own. You can only eliminate them when *everybody* changes their mind.

What do you think of the United Nations?

I try not to think of the United Nations. It seems to me that it's a very expensive gang of third-rate egotists who are all on power trips, blowing their little bugles. It's good for people to get things off their chest from time to time, but I think the United Nations is really pathetic. Perhaps over a period of time, some of these rinky-dink people will mature, and the organization might become a force for good in the world. Right now, they appear as little boys playing at being tin soldiers and grown-ups.

What do you think about the situation in Northern Ireland?

I go to Ireland a lot, although I don't go to the north. I think the Irish Republican Army is the result of a schizophrenic Irish soul. I don't think the Irish have ever really claimed back their power, their soul, their heart. They blame it on the English, and in a way they're right. The English definitely took over the Irish lands and disempowered the Irish people, but that was some time ago. Now in Ireland there is nothing stopping Irish men and women from standing up and grabbing their destiny. So I don't think the political situation in Ireland will ever really resolve itself until Ireland reclaims its own soul.

The other issue you have to consider is that a lot of the conflict is economic. It really doesn't have that much to do with religion; it's more about tribal breakdowns, arguments as to who will control the monopoly over the Belfast taxis, and that kind of stuff. It also has to do with Ireland's poverty. Of course, Ireland is currently one of the fastest-growing economies of all the European Communities, so as Ireland becomes more prosperous, the reasons for the intertribal warfare will wane.

It seems reasonable that Ireland should be reunited. However, within that, one has to accommodate the Protestants who were also born in Ireland. I'm glad I don't have to solve it myself.

What do you think will be the eventual outcome of the situation in the Middle East?

I don't think there is ever going to be an eventual outcome. The energy of the Israelis in the Middle East is a foreign energy in an Islamic/Arab land, and it will always be a thorns in the Arab side. However, the other thorn in the Arab side are the other Arabs, because they're always fighting among each other. I think there will be a perpetual state of flux in the Middle East.

Both Islam and Zionism are retrospective religions that look back to the medieval ways. It's comfortable for some people not to go forward any further, and instead go back to a previous time. However, in the long term, religions, philosophies, churches, and ideas have to move forward. Islam and Zionism will have to change and become less dogmatic, and more accepting and open. Of course as that happens, they will be able to live with each other better.

Do you think that people being angry with the government—for example, the "militia" in the USA, is just a passing fad, or that growing discontent will impact the government?

I do not think that people being angry with the government is a passing fad. One of the main reasons people are dissatisfied with the government is that, more often than not, the energy of the ordinary citizens has grown out of its docile acceptance of a military-style controlling body that dominates every aspect of their lives. That is why people are discontented with their governments. It's not the policies so much that causes the frustration, it's just the idea of somebody lording it over them.

We can't get rid of governments until people are self-sufficient. There are millions of citizens who will bitch about the government, but they are happy to cash the welfare checks as they come in. So we're going to be lumbered with governments for a little while longer.

However, you can be sure that the changing consciousness that has taken place since the late 1970s will continue to grow, and governments will become more aware of people's dissatisfaction. They will have to modify their actions somewhat, but it's my view that most of the adjustments will be cosmetic. It's very hard for a governing body that considers itself superior to pass laws that will abolish itself. It's going to be extremely interesting as we watch the governments going through the machinations of trying to sustain control over an increasingly liberated population.

The other interesting aspect to this topic is the government's central reason for existence, its *raison d'être*—money, and its ability to milk people and to control by financial clout. It has the kind of power that buys police forces and secret services and control mechanisms, surveillance, and armies. As our governments become increasingly bankrupt and self-indulgent, their ability to control will be decreased. Then we will be in an interesting situation whereby power will flow out of the government and back to the people. However, in that outflow of power will be a fragmentation that may cause some problems in the future.

If you had the opportunity to stand before all the world leaders, what would you say to them?

I don't know whether the wisdom of our planet ever rests with our leaders. It lies mostly with wise men and women who are not in the spotlight. I think by the very virtue of being on the podium, up on the stage, on the throne, head of all, they are usually complete idiots.

However, if I had a chance to stand before the world leaders, I would tell them they cannot continue the way they're going. Firstly, we have to have respect for our planet's well-being. Second, we have to have respect for the spiritual development of humanity. I'd also point out to the leaders that their thinking is old-fashioned, and that in order for them to stay in power, they have to let go and allow people to be. Then I think I would say, "You're fired!" because I don't see how the current leaders will change; they belong to an old evolution that is unnatural and outdated.

What we need is to change our leaders without hurting anyone and without any violence. The way these characters are running our planet into the ground is very bad karma. Eventually people will wake up and get very pissed off, and the leaders will be in serious trouble. I wouldn't want anyone to get hurt. I think I'd ask the leaders politely to quit while they safely can. With the change in spirituality and the velocity of the worldwide expansion in consciousness, the current system won't last.

As people's consciousness evolves, countries become less able to be governed. People just won't accept the manipulative control and power from the upper echelons. They don't regard the leaders as ambassadors capable of overseeing the real needs of society. Leaders no longer command as much respect, because most of them are sleaze-bags, liars, and phonies, and everybody knows it. If we had honorable leaders like Gandhi, I'm sure people would give them a lot more respect. But the fact is, in this stage of our evolution, we are pulling to us the kinds of leaders that reflect a selfish, ego-mad attitude that is part of the way society is.

If you were the personal advisor to the President of the United States, what would you tell him to do?

What I would like the president to do is to set the American people free from fear. I think most Americans see the government as a predator rather than a protector, so I would ask the president to loosen up the regulations and have a less adversarial attitude toward the citizens. I would definitely ask the president to change the law that allows the government to zoom in on people's bank accounts and assets. Governments take billions of dollars a year from their citizens, and they have to sue if they want it back. More often than not, the victims have no money left to hire lawyers, so the government steals money under the cover of the law.

If you could have dinner with the Pope, where would you take him, and what would you say to him?

I'd take him to an Italian restaurant because that's what he's probably used to, living in Rome as he does. The first question I would ask is why his religion is so full of restriction. I would suggest to him that he pass a few laws to liberate people. I think Catholicism comes off as a very tight-assed philosophy, and I think the goal of our humanity is to become more flowing, relaxed, laid-back, simpler, and easier. So I think I'd say, "Hey, Pope dude, lighten up."

Which sacred sites of the world have you visited, and which left the most profound impression on you?

I've been to most of the sacred churches, and the pyramids in Egypt. I haven't been to the sacred sites in South America or Mexico, such as Lake Titicaca, Machu Picchu, and Chichen Itza.

Uluru, formerly named Ayers Rock, in Australia, left a very profound impression on me. There is something about the vastness of the Australian desert and the ancient presence of the Aboriginal Dreamtime that I found extremely moving. I particularly enjoyed Uluru at night, when there were no people about. I could stand in the infinite stillness of the place and visualize myself stretching back through the history of Aboriginal people into their Dreamtime, into their imagination, and into the metaphysics of their sacred ways.

Of the sacred sites I have been to, I would say the Great Pyramid and Uluru are the two that have definitely touched me.

I read that you've been the equivalent of 97 times around the world. Is there anywhere you haven't been, and do you ever find yourself getting bored with places?

Yes, there are places I haven't been to. I've particularly avoided China because I'm not into their politics. I've never been to Japan, because I've never really had a reason to go there. I get bored with places very quickly, and I do not normally stay anywhere more than six or eight weeks at the most.

If you could visit any ancient civilization, live there for a year, learn all their mysteries, and come back and tell us about it, which would it be?

I would like to visit the ancient civilizations of South and Central America, such as the Maya and the Incas, or the societies that built the

Pyramids of Egypt. I don't believe the Great Pyramid of Giza was built by the Egyptians, and I would like to visit the people that did build it.

Do you think it is possible to visit ancient places like the Pyramids of Egypt, Volterra, Stonehenge, and other significant sites, and tune into the energy that was once there; or did the energy vanish along with the civilizations?

Some of the sacred sites still contain energy. Certainly, the Great Pyramid of Giza does. But I was in Volterra recently, the capital of the Etruscan empire, and I didn't get the impression that there was much of the old energy there—although I did have a strange sensation in my crown chakra as I was traveling up toward the site. Similarly, when I visited Stonehenge, it felt as flat as a tack to me. I have a feeling that in most of these places the energy has drained over time. But then again, I don't think that is really important. What is important is that they stimulate the imagination, so one can picture the world of the ancient Egyptians, Etruscans, Maya and so on.

The other point is that a lot of these places are crawling with so many tourists, people flogging postcards, and ice-cream vendors that it is hard to feel the energy even if it is present. When I visited the Pyramids, I went in the middle of the night. I had the Great Pyramid unlocked and went up into the King's chamber with a few of my friends. I was there for three or four hours on my own, so it was very different from wandering around with a bunch of tourists clicking cameras. If I could go down to Stonehenge and hang out there all night, I'm sure I would feel the power. But when you have to walk around with flocks of people, buses, and pollution, the energy is scattered and the sacredness is lost.

Do you have any theories on Atlantis?

I believe there is substantial evidence for the existence of civilizations such as Atlantis. I believe there have been civilizations on Earth just as technologically advanced, if not more so, than we are. Certainly, we know that when the last major snow melt took place approximately 8,000 years ago and the Ice Age ended, the seas rose almost 500 feet. London is about 20 feet above sea level, and I imagine New York is about the same. If you stand on the banks of the Hudson River and look down, you're not that high above water. It's not hard to figure out that there would be many civilizations under water if the seas suddenly rose 500 feet farther. So the idea that civilizations such as Atlantis were swamped by floods is not a point of mythology; it's a fact of geological history.

If you received in a meditation the knowledge that, without a doubt, a pole shift would occur on a certain date, where would you go?

First of all, I'd have to decide if I wanted to live in a post-pole-shift world. If the poles shifted, an awful lot of dust would be thrown into the air, and it might take 50 years for that dust to settle. So, do you want to live on a planet that isn't going to see the sun for two generations?

The other thing about a post-pole-shift existence is that we would really go back to the caveman stage, and I don't know if I could do "caveman"—all that rubbing of little sticks together and so forth would be a bit tedious. However, if I decided I wanted to survive a pole shift, I would definitely go high, rather than low; and I would go in rather than out. Let me explain. If a pole shifts quickly, it will cause tremendous tidal waves and winds of extreme velocity. You would have to be a long way from the beach, as coastal areas would be swamped, and you would need to be sheltered from the wind. So, probably high up and in the ground, inside a cave, would be the place to be.

Strangely enough, I think that Taos, New Mexico, would be a perfect place. If you lived in one of those earthships, the houses that they build there in the ground, you'd be very safe. It's unlikely that a tidal wave would come in from the Californian coast, travel 1,500 miles, then rise up a 7,000-foot plateau. Provided you were underground, you'd be safe from the wind. So I think if I knew the pole shift was happening next Thursday, I'd fly to New Mexico and hang out where I've always hung out.

Chapter Eight

WILDE ABOUT SPIRIT

In *Weight Loss for the Mind*, you write: "We have to believe in a god we can't see." Why is it so important to believe in a god?

In my view, the only thing that lasts forever is love, and the God Force is the highest manifestation of love that I'm aware of. I don't think one has to believe in a god, be it Jesus or Buddha or whatever, but I think one has to believe in the idea that the Light and the God Force permeate all things—because first, it's the reality; and second, everything else will disappear in the end as the Universe finally burns out. What we will be left with is only the light and love of God.

What has been the biggest spiritual challenge you have faced in your life?

The biggest challenge of my life hasn't really been a spiritual one, although it has been part of my spiritual quest. I always found spirituality, the disciplines of meditation and silence, very simple. My challenge was between activity and stillness. I always got off on the adrenaline trip of being active. That's why I've traveled around so much. In a way it was good, because I collected all the human experiences available to me. But sometimes, in a lot of activity, one is not really facing oneself. Activity is sometimes a way of masking the insecurities that lie deep inside, masking your consolidated sense of self, because you're always presenting yourself in a cloud of dust as your chariot screeches to a stop.

So my biggest spiritual challenge has been to give up going on the road as a metaphysical teacher, being in city after city—and forcing myself to quietly go within. It's a long way from the razzmatazz and the income of traveling and teaching. I must say the first few months of it were quite tough, but afterwards I actually liked the silence a lot better than the razzmatazz.

Which of your spiritual achievements are you most proud of?

What I have done is take complex ideas and explain them simply. I've been able to get spiritual, metaphysical information across to people without a lot of elitism and waffle. I feel that has been a good thing. The other thing I've been able to do in my seminars, especially many of the more complex ones, like *Warriors in the Mist*, was show people the existence of the etheric dimension. I took ordinary people with no particular training and showed them how to maneuver the etheric. I think that is an achievement, because I don't believe there are many teachers who know how to do that and are prepared to stick their neck out in that way.

Who are your favorite spiritual teachers?

I have a lot of respect for most of the people on the circuit teaching at the moment, and a number of them are dear friends. Deepak Chopra and Wayne Dyer are good mates, and the English healer Matthew Manning is a good pal.

Then there are a few teachers on the circuit who make me want to throw up. But I grin sweetly and wish 'em well. I must say if I was the God Force and I thought those characters were out there representing me, I'd quit.

Do you follow a "guru"?

I don't really have a guru I follow religiously, but there are many people whose writings I particularly admire. Of course Lao Tzu was one who influenced me, along with Emanuel Swedenborg.

Where would you call your spiritual home?

I think Taos, New Mexico, is my perpetual spiritual home, because it's where I've had the vision and the sense of belonging. However, Taos is changing rapidly and becoming a victim of the malaise that is spreading across America, with graffiti, violence, drugs, and all the other dysfunctional sicknesses that have been transported out of Los Angeles and New York. So there is a tinge of sadness when I go there because I see how much the energy of the place has changed.

You begin your book *The Force*, with a discussion on the spirit. When you talk about the spirit, are you referring to the soul, or is this something completely different?

I believe that the spirit and the soul are different. The Christian definition of the soul is, for all intents and purposes, the personality; a person's soul is the content of their personality, memories, and actions in this lifetime. In my opinion, spirit is a molecule of the divine light that is trapped inside the electromagnetic oscillations of the brain for the duration of the human lifetime, and it is only released after the brain stops. Spirit is eternal. I believe it has knowledge of itself prior to arrival on this Earth plane, and it will carry the memories of the soul (personality) after death.

Why does the energy of Camelot play such an important part in your teachings?

I've been keen on the legend of Camelot because in a world that's unraveling, where there seems to be an ever-increasing amount of nastiness, I like the idea of the chivalry and kindness of the Camelot legend. Also, I'm particularly interested in the idea of a group of people creating, from among themselves, a molecule of consciousness that is hidden away, protected, and guarded—a dimension that allows them to perceive beyond the influence and clutter of the global mind. It's been my intention to establish that same pristine, sacred place—a haven that people can retreat to in troubled times.

If you can establish a correctness in your life and teach that to others, the basic principles of the natural law will hold, no matter how much the ego dominates our planet and nastiness prevails. The legend of Camelot for me is a breach into another world—a softer, more spiritual, sensitive world, where respect, love, and compassion dominate; and perception is not limited to the wants and needs of the ego or the mundane restrictions of a three-dimensional life.

Sometimes it seems like the New Age movement has run out of ideas and is content with rehashing old ones. What do you think the future holds for the New Age movement?

I agree. The New Age movement has run out of steam. The same old ideas are being dressed in new clothes. The New Age trailed the flower-power phenomenon of the 1960s. Now, 30 years later, many facets of the New Age are beginning to run their course—such as crystal healing, channeling, shamanistic studies, gurus, meditation, and so on. It's the same for each and every person when they first turn within. There is a lot of inspiration, psychic activity, coincidences, excitement—and the exhilaration of turning away from the humdrum and embracing the infinite or spiritual self. After the initial flurry of activity, it goes quiet. It then becomes a long, silent journey until one reaches another phase of power and psychic activity.

The New Age has gone past its initial growth spurt and is now at a stage of consolidation. The term *New Age* really describes a change of consciousness, and for many people in many countries, that is already taking place. I think we're going to see the New Age move into countries that are still developing economically—such as Africa, Asia, and Eastern Europe—because the New Age is at a different stage of maturity in Western nations.

To track the progress of the New Age, you only have to look at the teachers. They come along and they're channeling "Bongo Dongo" or whatever, and it's all very exciting, new, and different. Yet when you look at the message of old "Bongo Dongo," the supposed spirit that comes from a Mayan temple or whatever, you'll find that the teaching is not really anything that dramatic. The message is basically to look within, believe in yourself, and be nice to your mum. You can see how many of the teachers, if they don't have a powerful inner journey of their own, tend to run out of things to say. Or they just keep repeating what they've already said. Or, in some cases, plagiarize other people's material.

What we're seeing is the consciousness movement beginning to plateau out. At the moment, being ill is fashionable. Half the planet is sick, and the other half are therapists. A lot of these diseases are really only brought on by the latest trend. They're generated to keep everybody happy by busily trying to fix up the past. That's not to negate the fact that people have had pain in their childhoods, and it's not to say that people haven't experienced various dysfunctions. The whole nature of family life is dysfunctional!

Over the next 10 or 20 years, we are going to go through a phase of dysfunctional extremes, with people trying to heal themselves just as zealously. Some of it will be over the top, but then that's just the way it is. Basically, I'm in favor of going within to heal the primal pain and dysfunctions of childhood.

So the reason the New Age does seem to be losing its impetus, having come up with all this stuff that is fairly obvious, is because the next journey has begun, the journey that explores the internal rather than external. It takes place deep within where the teaching comes from ourselves, from the serenity and silence where we can begin to perceive other realities, other spirit worlds, and embrace the dimension of angels.

What future do you see for the Catholic Church?

If the Catholic Church embraces the idea of female priests and eases the rules to allow male priests to marry, or creates some kind of cleric who takes holy orders and conducts services but is able to marry, then I think it has a good future. In particular, if the church opens up to women, then it has quite a strong future, especially in developing countries where people are more into the simplicity of a religious philosophy than looking within. I think if it continues to exclude women and discriminate against homosexuals and others who could possibly act as priests, then gradually the Catholic Church will become a very marginalized institution.

What will be the biggest spiritual challenge in the new millennium?

I think the biggest spiritual challenge in the new millennium will be trying to sustain a spiritual stance of love, kindness, and benevolence in what will be a chaotically imbalanced society. If you haven't figured out where you're going to retreat to in the first few years of the next century and onwards, you should start thinking about it. You're going to want a bit of distance from the run-of-the-mill energy of the collective evolution

How can we help usher a spiritual revolution on Earth at a faster rate? It frustrates me when I see and experience the ignorance that rules our planet.

I'm working on a novel that discusses the concept of the "professional waiter." The professional waiter is a person who can wait inside their infinity, opposed to an amateur waiter who waits inside their emotions. So an amateur waiter can wait for 20 minutes or so, but in the end their personality dominates and they get impatient. The professional waiter is immortal and can just wait forever. So we don't have to do anything to create a spiritual revolution on our planet, other than embrace spiritual ideas inside our hearts, bypassing our fears and attempting to live this new evolution.

Our systems are categorically, absolutely, bound to collapse. They have absolutely no place they can go other than fall apart. Why? Because until they fall apart, we can never set our people free, and the desire in the hearts and souls of people is freedom. At the moment, most people can't embrace freedom because it is scary, so they are playing freedom "nip and tuck." But once they understand what freedom is all about, the systems will disappear, possibly by the next generation. We don't have to do anything—just wait and watch the systems crumble.

In *Whispering Winds of Change*, you say that if the time was right, any one of us could "walk up to the system and take the crown back. That's exactly what we're going to do. We just have to know we can do it." Do you still believe that, and if so, when is it going to happen?

When Joan of Arc crowned the Dauphin as king, France was in a state of political turmoil, so it was a possibility. Right now our institutions are only changing as much as they have to. Recent years have seen a strengthening in the economy, and therefore a strengthening in the ego's position in the grip of tick-tock, so to speak. So I don't think this would be the time to go in and sack the government. But in *Whispering Winds of Change*, I was stating that the power lies with the people. As the old adage goes, "There's nothing more powerful than an idea whose time has come." This idea of change is in the state of becoming.

I like the idea of moving into a new dimension of existence on Earth, but how can I prepare myself for change? Already I see the world hurling toward virtual collapse, and it seems rather daunting.

I like watching things crumble, especially when what is crumbling is the institutional, patriarchal dominance of people. As you watch it crumbling, rather than being scared and wondering whether the insurance company will pay up, know that the true insurance is in your energy and in your ability. Your guarantee lies in your skills and enthusiasm, in your love for your family and friends, and in your courage. What will happen? You'll be fine. As you begin to move away from the evolution of people, you move away from tribal emotion and its level of energy. You will then be able to walk through the middle of a riot and nobody will notice you. Just continue to believe that your life is sacred, and the upcoming changes won't seem so daunting.

In your book *Whispering Winds of Change*, you talk about the concept of spiritual "fringe dwellers," people who have left or are leaving the system. What do you mean by "the system"?

We live in a funny world, a changing world that's not really designed for us. There are millions of people on the planet today who don't fit comfortably into the way society has been structured. The reason they don't fit is because systems have been devised. They were created under the terms of the patriarchal/religious authority whereby royalty, aristocracy, church leaders, land owners, and what eventually became governments, *controlled* the people. This system was established centuries ago, yet when we look at Western democracies, we can see that they are built on massive amounts of restriction. There still isn't any space for real individuality, creativity, or disagreement. We are completely free on one condition and one condition only—that we don't want to do anything.

As long as we want to do bugger all for the rest of our lives, we are going to be free. But if we actually want to do something, then we're not free. Why? Because there are a million rules that cover anything we want do. If you want to be an architect, there are a million rules about how to be an architect. You can't just scribble a building down on the back of an envelope—I have, but then my policy is, "stuff the rules." Interestingly enough, you would imagine that, as we advance, our societies would become more liberated and suitable for humans to live in. But they're not, because they are built on ego-based precepts that are crumbling and falling apart. The result is that the system is becoming increasingly rule oriented.

I didn't quite grasp the concept of fringe dwellers in *Whispering Winds of Change.* Can you explain?

I define "spiritual fringe dweller" as any person whose heart and soul has left the system. Anyone who looks at these political, religious, and financial systems and says, "This isn't for me. I need freedom; I need to breathe." We are at the forefront of this phenomenon. Many of us are conjuring up the courage to leave—and leaving what you know is very difficult to do. That's what holds a lot of people back, this idea of leaving the prison they have created for themselves. But fringe dwellers are saying, "Hey, we don't accept. We're not going to necessarily blow the whole system up, although we might like to. But what we are saying is that we want a world that is organized for the people. We want a world where we can organize ourselves into small communities. We want a world that looks after our planet, a world based on love and fairness, not on political manipulation and hatred. We want a world built on conservation not consumption."

Why do people become fringe dwellers? Is it a choice?

People become fringe dwellers because they take on a new set of values, so it is a conscious choice. However, sometimes people are fringe dwellers because they had parents who distanced themselves from society's standards. The whole process of distancing your consciousness from the evolution of tick-tock is really a by-product of detachment—seeing the present problems in the context of the evolution of humanity and having compassion for people and for the pain and anguish society goes through, but not necessarily buying into the emotion.

Have we any obligations as fringe dwellers?

As fringe dwellers, the only obligation we really have is setting a good example, showing other people that—with courage and tenacity and a certain amount of self-discipline—you can sustain yourself while remaining distant from the system and without falling apart economically, spiritually, or physically. Each person who walks away from the system represents one grain of sand removed from the pillars that support the old institutions.

The obligation of the fringe dweller is to demonstrate, through love and compassion, that there is an evolution outside conformity and tick-tock. The fringe dweller also has the ability to show fearlessness—and in that fearlessness offer hope and courage to others who may be a little timid or insecure about the idea of embracing freedom, and emotionally removing themselves from the system.

Is it possible that fringe dwellers could reach a point where they do not operate out of the tick-tock of society, but eventually form a new, alternative tick-tock that is just as imprisoning?

Yes, of course. You can already see that in the parts of the New Age movement that are wrapped in dogma, rules, righteous spirituality, and a holier-than-thou attitude. Many New Agers look down their noses at you if you dare to suggest something slightly different. So I think in the future the new consciousness could, and probably will, form a new type of tick-tock, although slightly higher on the consciousness ladder. I don't think it really matters as long as consciousness keeps rising. What we're going to see is good spurts of conscious awakening, and then a slowing down while ideas consolidate, people hang out on the plateau, and then another spurt. So we just have to be patient and think in terms of thousands of years and not just a decade or two.

As someone who considers themselves a fringe dweller, I sometimes feel sorry for those who have not yet grasped the fact that we are spiritual beings. Is there something I should be doing to help them?

Your responsibility is to become strong, to stand for others and show the way, to look the system in the eye and when it tries to manipulate you, say "No." One of the greatest affirmations you can create for yourself is to look in the bathroom mirror, imagine you are looking at the patriarchal institutional control of our planet, and fearlessly say, "Stuff you, and your little dog, too." Try it. Because at some point we have to make a stand. It only takes one Gandhi. It only takes one man or one woman to put the foot on the other side of this emotional line and say to the system, "You're finished."

In *Whispering Winds of Change*, you also talk about "spiritual terrorists." You somehow make them responsible for changing the evolution of the globe. Could you explain who they are? How do you see them changing planet Earth's evolution?

I refer to spiritual terrorists as those people who are quietly creating a metaphysical/spiritual/psychological change in the world. Rules and regulations imposed on society are there to sustain the status quo, to impose control through terror, and fear of retribution. Society will not accept anything that is contradictory to the status quo, the power base, or the government. However, while the institutions that create these structures are theoretically chasing after anarchists, terrorists, and drug dealers, the foundation of our society is being pulled away from underneath them by the fact that there are loads of people going out there and creating a change of consciousness. Spiritual terrorists, through their own metaphysical, spiritual, and psychological journeys, are challenging the status quo.

I see nonviolent spiritual terrorists being responsible for the change in the evolution of the planet. We need a system that's less hateful, militant, and violent—and more caring.

When you talk about the etheric in *The Quickening*, you refer to it as a hidden world, but if it permeates all living things, how can it be hidden?

I refer to the etheric as a hidden world because it is really beyond normal perception, yet it's there like electricity is there. It does permeate all living things, however, and perhaps it permeates the entire cosmos. I'm just recently coming around to the idea that perhaps the etheric *is* the entire cosmos, and that what we see as stars and galaxies are the external manifestation of higher-dimensional etheric reality expressed in a lower-dimensional 3-D state.

Once you begin to slow down your brainwaves through meditation and you enter a trance state, you're able to feel the etheric. A simple technique is to get yourself into a relaxed position, lie down north to south, and as you enter into a deep meditative/trance state, attempt to move your legs down through the floor so that your etheric body is now at right angles to your physical body. It isn't as hard as it sounds, and it is the first step toward a full out-of-body experience.

Why do you feel it is important to stretch your etheric like you teach us to do in your trance tapes and meditations?

There are three reasons why stretching the etheric is important. First of all, in stretching the etheric, you enliven it. It has more space and it can move faster. Normally, the etheric doesn't move much at all, except as a reaction to emotions.

Second, you begin to understand that *you are* the etheric and you can direct it with your will. You can learn to move the etheric outside the physical body while you are still wide awake, and you can get it to do something across the room, and come back. As I mention in the *Trance States* tapes, in stretching the etheric and creating more space within it, you can begin to induce the out-of-body state where you are close to other dimensions, hovering between this world and others.

Finally, stretching the etheric allows you to understand that you can empower yourself through the mind and force of will.

Reading your books really stimulates me into seeking a more spiritual life. I would like to believe that one day I will reside in the etheric, but I get the impression that it is a very long and involved process. How long does it really take, and do I have to do things like take cold baths at four every morning? I don't think I could really go that far.

The beauty of this process is that it takes no time at all. Really, you can do it in about 15 minutes. Now, if you are a counselor, never tell it to your customers. But if you're not a counselor or a therapist, you can do it in about 15 minutes. And it is just a matter of understanding that you aren't your personality, your ego, or your physical body; you are spirit. Taking a cold bath will not help unless you are feeling incredibly horny, or it is something you believe will quiet your ego. I used to go walking in the forest at 4 A.M. but that was something that helped me on my own journey. It really is up to you how you want to learn to resist the ego's whining.

What do you think are the most important spiritual or metaphysical books ever written?

Without a shadow of a doubt, they would be the Bible and the Koran. Even though those messages now seem somewhat stilted and out of date to many, Christianity imposed a discipline upon people. From it came the rule of law, order, and the sanctity of human life. The Koran similarly has imposed a code of conduct upon the people of Islam. I think it would be a barbaric world if those ideals had not been incorporated into our cultures. I think one could also include the teachings of the Buddha. Those three religions—Buddhism, Christianity, and Islam—would cover 80 percent of the planet, so I would definitely consider those to be the most powerful spiritual writings.

Chapter Nine

WILDE ABOUT THE PSYCHIC WORLD

WILDE ABOUT THE PSYCHIC WORLD

Who are we, Stuart? Are we a spirit once we leave Earth, or are we a spirit now? I know you've talked about the "etheric" as a term for describing who we are, but I'd like to know what you really mean. It's difficult to get a grasp on the whole idea of being a spirit when everything we do revolves around a physical existence.

As my friend Wayne Dyer says, "You are not a human being having a spiritual experience; you are a spiritual being having a human experience." That's an idea that is only just catching on, because the five billion or so people on this planet are physical egos having a physical-ego experience. They haven't even gotten to the idea of being a human having a spiritual experience.

When we come to this spiritual plane, we rent, so to speak, a physical body from God. Some of us are renting from Rent-a-Dent, some of us from Cadillac Rentals, some of us from Rolls-Royce rentals, and that is the first restriction we experience. If you've ever had an out-of-body experience, you will know that the second you come out of your body and roll away, you will feel a sense of lightness. When you think about it, your personality doesn't even come to Earth. You may think that is a ridiculous statement, but it's true. You begin with a blank slate and you start to create memories. As you create memories, you gradually create a personality. Your memories are hovering between your ears. So, if you stand on your head, your personality is still the thickness of your skull away from the Earth plane. There is no way to get this personality to land. Everybody thinks this life is so important, so magnificent, and so immediate. Yet the real you isn't even here and never will be. The real you never comes to Earth; you're near to it, hovering above it, but you're not actually here.

Your subconscious exists in a timeless dimension relating to the 3-D finite world via the intellect. The subconscious is where your personality and memory lie, so in effect it is the storehouse of your soul. Because the subconscious is timeless, you could say that your soul is never here on Earth, as it exists in the infinite timeless dimension of the subconscious mind rather than the finite dimension of the intellect and the 3-D Earth plane.

This is why I say that the "real you" never comes to Earth for it is always outside the space/time continuum, hovering between your ears in a finite body operating through a finite 3-D intellect, yet resting all the while in its infinite state, timeless and immortal.

How do you know that astral traveling, out-of-body experiences, psychic abilities, and so on are not just a figment of your imagination when you experience them?

You don't. Certain astral traveling is definitely a figment of your imagination. I think you can easily tell with psychic abilities because it's just a matter of being right or wrong. If you get a psychic flash about something, you can check your facts and you will know whether or not you've imagined it. As far as an out-of-body experience [OBE] is concerned, I don't think it's imagination if you feel yourself outside your body. What I've discovered is that your feelings are outside with you, so you can actually go and touch things in an out-of-body state. You'll put your hand up against a wall and it will feel slightly stiff, slightly resistant, because that's how you know it to be. When you push through the wall, your hand will go through it.

Yes, one could say that all of this is part of your imagination, but I don't think the imagination is so sophisticated that it could invent all these things. The other thing that is interesting about near-death experiences and OBEs is that people describe exactly the same phenomena, the same methodology, the same experiences. If it was just people's imaginations, you would get a lot of contradictions and differences. We seem to have a pretty solid consensus as to what happens when you come out of your body. So I would say that it's not imagination in many cases. I've been involved in this area of research for many years and I've had many, hundreds in fact, confirmations of the existence of other dimensions and parallel worlds.

Do you see any real benefit in trying to contact the dead?

I've dealt with this a lot in my books. In the English spiritualist churches, the mediums will contact your dead granny, and so on. What I discovered was that if your granny was thick when she was alive, then she'll be thick when she's dead. However, I can see how people who are grieving the loss of a loved one may derive a tremendous support, love, and emotional benefit by feeling that the spiritual medium has made contact.

I must say, I've been to some spiritualist churches in England where the mediums were absolutely brilliant. They would get impressions from some departed spirit, deliver the information to the audience, and it was pretty impressive. I think if it helps people, why not?

There is a downside to contacting the dead, and that's when you start contacting evil or demonic astral entities. That can cause you a bit of worry. But I think if you're loving in your heart and your intentions are good, then there's nothing wrong with it.

What do you think of Wicca, and do you believe in magic?

I don't have any problem with Wicca (witchcraft) and magic. Magic is really the technology of visualization, using the power of the mind and sacred rituals. True Wicca, which is witchcraft that is practiced for higher spiritual growth and follows the path of light, is fine.

I suppose there is an occult connotation with magic. The idea of black magic and conjuring up demons is what bothers people. But if you can perform magic and your craft is positive, then all well and good. I've met a few satanic characters on my travels that conjure up demons in order to control or abuse other people. All of that is highly devious. Usually the magicians and witches involved in this sort of stuff come to a grisly end. But then they would probably come to a grisly end if they didn't get into magic, because those I've met are nasty little people. I don't think their nastiness is the magic; I think the magic is one way they can express their nastiness. If they weren't into magic, they would still be nasty people, and they would abuse, infringe, violate, rip off, or psychically attack people. I'm not that keen on those kinds of characters, but we do need both light and dark.

Is it an infringement to cast spells to help people if they haven't specifically asked you to do so? Will it interfere in their evolutionary process?

Yes, in my view it is a tremendous infringement, and I would suggest you don't interfere. I think that if you do interfere with others, it will detract from your own evolutionary process because you'll get stuck at whatever level you decide to get involved. I can't see how that would help you.

How long does it take to develop the ability to penetrate into other dimensions?

I think we exist as multidimensional beings all the time, so the time it takes you to penetrate it is zero, because you're perpetually in it. The perception of it takes a little while, because one somehow has to move from intellect into the infinite self. I talk more about it in my tape series and book *Infinite Self: 33 Steps to Reclaiming Your Inner Power*. It's basically just quieting and disciplining the mind. If you can entrance the mind and get down to the theta level of four cycles a second without falling asleep, gradually you will perceive yourself moving across different dimensions, and you will eventually see inside those dimensions.

I believe that in just thinking about the world that is beyond the mirror, you place yourself there. It's much like a child in the womb. Once it's born into the worldly dimension, it develops sight, touch, hearing, and taste, and eventually it becomes functional in another dimension and can evolve in it.

I believe you are a personality that comes from a group of memories. These memories are housed in the subconscious that you've acquired so far in this lifetime. It's the idea that you can create another evolution, beyond the veil, beyond the mirror, whereby you place a spiritual identity on that side, and it evolves with the memories you have so far. It's just a matter of hiving off molecules of oneself, and placing them in various dimensions so they might evolve elsewhere. In the end, I think that's probably what the Higher Self does.

The Higher Self is a molecule of memory of higher consciousness. It somehow enters into the physical body, and becomes present in the physical body, let's say, as a molecule of golden light. It places itself in the babe and evolves through that physical being. The being is also going through an emotional evolution, a psychological evolution, a physical evolution, and an intellectual evolution. The Higher Self is there recording all these evolutions and creating one more evolution for itself—the collection of all these other evolutions the child will acquire in his/her lifetime.

So if the Higher Self can enter a physical body and evolve that way, I'm wondering if—once we have a group of memories in the mind—through concentration we may be able to hive a molecule of ourselves into another dimension and evolve there. Or perhaps hive ourselves off to evolve in another physical body, simultaneous to the one we already have. I can't say I have that particular technology down pat in my mind, but it certainly bears thinking about.

What is the difference between the sixth sense, intuition, and psychic abilities?

They're all related to each other. A lot of the psychic abilities come from mental transfer. You'll be with a person, and a thought will jump across from them, enabling you to pick up the direction they're going in their life, or some aspect of their thinking or their desires. A lot of psychic information is transferred like that.

Intuition often comes from the subliminal nature of perception. Sometimes you can pick up information subliminally, and a day later it will flash in your mind as intuition. But, in fact, it's not really a supernatural knowing; it's more a subtle knowing. The example I've given in the past is that you might subliminally pick up on some fine noise in the engine of your car. Then you'll get in your car two or three days later and think, *My God, we're going to break down.* You think it's intuition when, in fact, you heard it in the subtle change in the engine noise, which indicated some technical problem or malfunction.

The sixth sense is all-knowing. As you discipline your life, exit the evolution and emotion of the Earth plane, and embrace the infinite self within, you become more connected to people and the whole energy of this evolution. As you practice pulling information and ideas to you, you tune more into the sixth sense. In the end, you know what people are thinking and feeling, and you know where things are going. So the sixth sense is cool, because it saves you a lot of trouble, and it makes you wise.

Many people suggest that it is more advantageous to trust one's inner guidance, or superconscious than information received psychically from the spirit world. But how do we know our inner guidance knows more than the inner guidance of a spirit being?

I think it's easy to get hung up on definitions between one's inner guidance, one's superconscious, one's Higher Self, psychic phenomena, and spirit worlds. Any information that comes to you, from wherever it comes to you, if it makes sense and is correct, then all's well and good. If it doesn't make sense and is woo-woo, if it tells you to sell everything and give your money to some weirdo charity, then watch out. I think it's very much a matter of not getting hung up. If it feels good, step forward gingerly, and if you don't know, don't go.

What is the relationship between the chakras and the etheric?

The word *etheric* comes from the Greek word meaning "to blaze." It is the light that emanates from us and is visible to the naked eye using the peripheral vision. The real you is actually inside the etheric, and it's where your feelings lie. Everything else is not you.

The word *chakra* is Sanskrit for "spinning wheel." Certainly chakras feel like wheels, or openings. If you imagine water going down a plughole in a bath, that's the best way I can describe the chakras. The chakras allow energy to flow in and out of the etheric body, but I am not as yet an expert on the technology of the system. One thing I've discovered over the years is that the throat chakra is the public speaker's chakra. Sometimes I'd be up on stage and I'd feel the throat chakra opening, and it felt like I had a big melon under my chin. I'd feel terribly odd because I'd be talking to an audience with my chin pointing slightly upwards, looking rather weird.

One technique I use to open the chakras, which I believe is different from other teachings, is I visualize my concentration at the root of the spine, and I come up through the center of the body and open the chakras from the inside out. It's like visualizing oneself up the middle of one's personage and pushing out through the chakra, rather than opening it from the outside. I visualize a pair of etheric eyes looking out through this hole where the chakra is.

What happens if you open the chakras and forget to close them?

If you open the chakras and forget to close them, it does make you vulnerable, especially when you're out in public. It is possible for energies to follow you up the street and attach themselves to you. It is not a clever idea to open the chakras and wander around where unwanted energies may enter.

If your chakras are open and you're in trance, especially if you're in an out-of-body state, occasionally astral entities will show up and taunt you or attempt to terrorize you. At the beginning, this can be very frightening; however, as you gain more expertise, you feel more confident and you know that the astral entities can't actually do you any harm. The stock standard defense is to look the entity in the eye and tell it to piss off. If you threaten them, they will usually turn and flee.

Can animals see and understand the etheric of humans?

Yes. I'm absolutely convinced that animals can see and understand the etheric of humans, and I'm convinced they feel energy. You can also find animals in the etheric dimension. On one occasion I was in trance and I became aware of a dog over to my left. It was a German shepherd. The dog walked over to me, nudged my leg, and walked away again. So, not only can animals see the etheric, but there are animals out there in the etheric dimension.

Whether you can see the etheric of an animal depends on its size. It's easy to see the etheric of larger animals like dogs. I can't say for certain whether an ant has an etheric because it's too small to see. But generally you can see the etheric of anything bigger than about the size of a mouse.

How can wearing gemstones and crystals on the body affect the etheric?

I'm not sure about gemstones, but definitely crystals on the body do affect the etheric. The one that affects the etheric the most is lodestone, which was used by the Druids and early mystics. It has a fantastic pulling energy because it's magnetic. In fact, the ancient mariners used lodestone for rudimentary compasses back in the old days. I can't say I can tell you exactly what the stones do, but I've used lodestone a lot, and I believe it to be effective.

What's the point of learning to see people's auras?

In one sense, seeing someone's aura really doesn't do much for you. Their aura or etheric body is an external manifestation of their life. If you're not particularly interested in someone's innermost feelings, why would seeing their aura be of interest?

Seeing the etheric comes about gradually as you develop yourself metaphysically. It's like you're blind, then one day you can see. It's just an affirmation of the journey. I don't know if the etheric has much to do with most people's evolution. But if you happen to be trotting along, evolving, and suddenly there it is, fine. You're seeing and learning about something different.

One thing that has helped me a lot is that while watching people's auras in the street, it always reminds me that we live in a multidimensional, spiritual world—not just a physical world of bodies, streets, and cars. So that's the point for me.

What do you mean when you talk about the "subtle body"?

We already know that you are more than just a physical body because you're a personality with thoughts and emotions. But beyond that, I have discovered through my investigations into the etheric web, that we are, also, in fact, a subtle body.

The subtle body or etheric web is where feelings exist. In fact, I have recently come to the conclusion that a human being has no capacity to feel other than in the etheric web. Don't confuse feelings with sensations. If I whack my hand, that's a sensation, an electrical message running to the brain. Your emotions—which the ego makes into an incredible, grandiose, important thing—are also sensations. They result from the sensation of having your ego either contradicted or agreed with.

Your real feelings, your spirit, the real energy of what you are, is inside the golden light that is blazing inside of you. You can certainly use your mind to *think* an emotion into being, but where you *feel* it is in the etheric, or subtle, body.

If you were trained, could you put thoughts into other people's minds?

Over the years, I've come to believe that there is only one consciousness that links all of us. So I don't believe you really need training to put thoughts into other people's minds—it's an ongoing and natural process.

Our separation from each other is an illusion created by the ego/personality. We're all inside the one molecule of consciousness, the global mind—we're interconnected. In order to be aware of other people's thoughts, or to project your thoughts powerfully to them, you have to create an uncluttered mind. So you have to turn down the mental radio of your inner dialogue so you'll hear the whispers coming through the walls from the skulls of others.

How can you stop people projecting thoughts into your mind?

Psychic intrusion is a problem because we all exist inside the same mind, so it's difficult to protect yourself from other parts of yourself. Furthermore, if you are a sexually active being, it's impossible to ward off the sexuality projected toward you. You can only stop that incoming sexual energy if you are celibate.

The best way to protect yourself from the negative thoughts of others is to look deep within yourself and process your own negative thoughts and feelings. You have to look at your shadow — all those resentments and hatreds and ill will and the anger that may lurk deep within. If you have nothing but love in your heart, little can affect you. Also, if you believe in yourself, and your etheric is strong and lively, most thoughts that carry ill feeling, will bounce off you.

For some time now I have been trying to figure out what process and technologies might work best for etheric protection. How do you stop people leaning up against your subtle body or penetrating it? In the case of people who report UFO abductions—which in most cases I believe are etheric abductions—I'm interested in how they can help protect themselves from unwanted intrusions, losing time and all the other terrifying phenomena reported by the abductees. I wish I could say I have the answer. I don't as yet have a solid methodology to offer.

I have been on the path for about five years now. I've left my tick-tock job and am involved in various meditation groups. One morning in a meditation I suddenly found myself in another dimension. I saw a figure wearing a long robe with a hood, standing in a doorway. There were no walls and no door, just a doorway, with a thick mist covering the ground. There was a strong white light behind the figure, and I could not see its face. I have never experienced anything like this before, and am longing for it to happen again. What do you think it means, and how can I make it happen again?

In my perception, the energy on the other side of the doorway presents itself in images and visions that are understandable to a human being. You see that which you will understand. The figure covered with a long robe, the mist, and the white light is archetypal of what one might expect to see. You cannot make it happen again. It's a symbol that says, here is an evolution, a guiding light, a power that you can evolve to. It is faintly possible you may see the figure once or twice more, but you can't make it happen. It's there to inspire and show you that the journey is infinite, and your progress has been substantiated.

I find myself inexplicably drawn to voodoo and the occult. What would you advise?

Occult, in the European sense of the word, is a very holy, very righteous, very disciplined science. As the word is understood in America, *occult* means "black magic." The study of any of these ancient wisdoms is okay, providing it leads you along the path of light.

I've never been exposed to the Caribbean voodoo, although I did notice there was a lot of black magic in Jamaica when I was there. The only voodoo I have been even marginally exposed to was voodoo practitioners in Baltimore, Maryland. They weren't my cup of tea. They were very weird, manipulative, and dark.

Like anything, you can take a look at it, but if it doesn't feel right, then it's time to split.

In much of your work, you talk about the Thousand-Day Climb, the Plane of Desolation, and the doorway into another dimension. Is it possible to experience all three at the same time, or is it a logical progression from one to the other?

I suppose it is possible; however, that's not how I experienced it. The Thousand-Day Climb really describes the psychological turning point where one becomes fed up with tick-tock, and turns within. Experience tells us that it takes approximately a thousand days for a person to come out of the mundane consciousness of tick-tock into a higher plane of awareness.

The Plane of Desolation is the point of one's inner journey after the Thousand-Day Climb, where many of one's old tick-tock values have died, but one's spiritual sight is not yet completely open. This period feels desolate to the spiritual traveler who is journeying within. It is a long plane that one travels across, heading inwards.

Eventually, you find the doorway to another dimension that is at the end of the Plane of Desolation, so it has seemed a logical progression to me. It's not only gauged through inner distance but also in external time. It took me well over ten years. But that's not to say somebody else couldn't do it in ten minutes. Who knows?

Does the journey of the Thousand-Day Climb that you discuss in your books and tapes increase your sexual drive?

As you exit the sluggish world of tick-tock and turn within, you begin to develop more energy, especially if you take on the kinds of disciplines I suggest in my book and tape series, *Infinite Self: 33 Steps to Reclaiming Your Inner Power*. The etheric—where your deeper feelings lie—begins to oscillate faster. In that heightened oscillation, the sex drive does increase. In addition, the kundalini is awakened and begins to move up the spine. So, the heightening of awareness and the speeding up of your etheric's oscillation can create an increase in your sex drive.

Moreover, as you raise your energy and oscillate faster and faster, you become more sexually attractive to other people, so you may be exposed to more sexual energy being projected toward you.

However, some people have the opposite response, and during the journey they close down sexually, as they find it simpler to concentrate on their spiritual quest than be involved in the complication of sexual relationships.

Have you experimented much with lucid dreaming?

Yes, I have done a lot of lucid dreaming. I make it fairly simple and easy for myself by going into lucid dreaming via meditation. Lucid dreaming is being conscious of dreaming while you are in the dream state. So you can either wake yourself up during the dream, or allow the dream to begin while you're still conscious. That's the route I take, and I find it exhilarating. The flying dreams are the most fun.

I remember one where I was moving along a hedgerow on the edge of a field. I would have been about six feet above the ground and moving at about 25 miles an hour toward a ruined castle. The flight lasted only about 20 seconds, but it was so exhilarating to know I could fly. The ruined castle I could see in the distance is, in fact, a famous castle in Norfolk, England.

Do you believe in angels?

I think the whole angel thing nowadays has been a bit overdone. Everybody would like you to believe that the angels are sitting in your front room, waiting to serve you at the flick of an angelic wing. My definition of angels is that they are positive spirit entities of another world. So yes, I do believe in angels, and I believe that they permeate our dimension.

Do you believe in the elementals—that is, the gnomes, undines, salamanders, and sylphs?

Yes, I do. I definitely believe in the power of nature, and I believe in the forces of earth, water, fire, air, and ether. The elementals are the divinity of each element personified as a particular character.

I did have one experience of seeing gnomes, which was like an inner-eye vision. But simultaneous with seeing it with my inner eye, my eyes were open—so I had the impression that it was outside of me and inside of me at the same time.

I was walking in a forest down a mossy bank, which was almost like a tunnel. It was very dark, and here and there little specks of sunlight flickered through. I saw half-a-dozen little gray objects out in front of me, about the size of turkeys. They had their backs to me, but they seemed to be very large pigeon-colored turkeys pecking on the ground. But what was interesting was that they had smooth backs of that beautiful dove-colored gray, and pale black lines on either side of their spine.

As I got closer to these beings, they all simultaneously stood up. I could see that, in fact, they weren't birds, but gnome like characters about two-and-a-half feet tall. They had little round gray bodies, quite long arms, and bony features on their faces. I wasn't aware of them having any facial hair, or hair on their heads. They weren't wearing any clothes, but I don't remember them having any genitalia. They were beckoning for me to approach their world. But I looked at them and, as sweet as they were, I wasn't so keen on their world. I just bade them farewell and went on my way.

I do believe in the spirits of nature, and I believe we can call them up through our hearts. You can direct air into your life, you can use the freshness of water, the power of fire, the grounding and nurturing of the earth, and the mysticism and metaphysics of the ether. We are all of those elements and more. The Druids I know who live out in the forests are very aware of them.

What are your thoughts on the connection between spirituality and psychedelic drugs?

Almost all cultures in the world have a heritage or teaching about psychedelic or psychotropic drugs. It has been a part of spiritual evolution for years. The good aspect of psychedelic drugs is that they're not, for the most part, particularly habit-forming. Certainly, psychotropic drugs such as mescaline, peyote, and so on are not usually addictive.

The reason these drugs became popular in Western society in the 1960s, and have since become so much a part of modern culture, is that the old, rigid vision of the world—what I refer to in my writings as the "tick-tock" vision—is dying. Tick-tock is the mundane rhythm of ordinary "nine-to-five" consciousness in which much of the population exists. It's not that it isn't any good; it's just that the era of conformity and restraint is over. People need more freedom. Through psychedelic and psychotropic drugs, people have been able to expand their awareness and experience an alternative state of consciousness, something that has been practiced in Eastern cultures for centuries. If you want to take these drugs to increase your awareness, you need to be a very disciplined and spiritual person.

I'm more in favor of the psychotropic drugs than their psychedelic counterparts. I've only ever had a couple of LSD trips in my life, and I saw lots of lovely pictures, but not much more than that. But mescaline, peyote, and the San Pedro cactus of South America literally take you to the doorway of other worlds and show you things you've never seen before. So I think it is one way of expanding your consciousness. The main concern I would have is if you're doing it on a regular basis; like anything, you can lose touch with reality.

Have you ever been into the divination sciences such as astrology, tarot, I Ching, and so on? Do you feel they are effective tools for spiritual growth?

I've never been that much into astrology and tarot. I've read the *I Ching* and used it. They are very effective tools, as they allow the practitioner to focus, and help people enormously. Anything that works is fine by me.

Chapter Ten

WILDE ABOUT THE UNIVERSE

Do you believe in UFOs?

I do believe in UFOs. In fact, when I was a little boy, my father used to take me out into the bush in Ghana, West Africa, where we used to live, and we would look for UFOs in the sky. He would meet with other UFO enthusiasts and subscribe to the odd UFO magazine, such as there were in those times. So I was brought up in a family of people who believed in them.

However, my emphasis in this lifetime has been on the inner journey, the spiritual and metaphysical journey back to God, rather than worrying so much about the external, and the denizens of other galaxies. In recent times, though, I've somewhat changed my view because the whole UFO thing has become so prevalent. In September 1996, I saw my first UFO in New Mexico. I was giving a seminar up in the mountains in Taos, and half a dozen of us watched a UFO fly up a valley and hover above us. It was there for several days, which is incredibly odd. A week later I saw the same craft make more or less the same movement. However, this time I was watching from a place in southern England called Dorset, near the old Roman town of Dorchester. Bit by bit the UFO began drawing lines in the sky, and I felt it was trying to communicate with us.

Since then I have seen a whole lot of strange flights in the sky all over the world. Recently there was a UFO over the roof of my house at a height of about 500 feet. It was metallic silver, and it hovered in the air, wafting back and forth, a bit like a leaf might. It stayed for a few minutes and then flew off at a slow speed, 20 to 30 miles per hour toward the southwest.

So I do believe in UFOs and extraterrestrial existences, mainly because our Milky Way is enormous, and it's only one of billions of galaxies out there. There are hundreds of thousands of stars that are like our sun, so there is absolutely no reason why those stars shouldn't have planets that are at the correct temperature, distance, or age to support life. Of course, we know that our physical plane is made of helium and hydrogen, and that's pretty much it. So the idea that the constituents we find on our planet haven't come together anywhere else in the universe is ludicrous in my view.

I also believe in the transdimensional nature of UFOs. If ETs can transcend space/time and travel in the fifth dimension, then they may not only be denizens of another place. It could be also that much of the phenomena we see are spiritual beings that have the ability to move in and out of our reality. So I think we possibly have an external nuts-and-bolts UFO phenomena, and an inner metaphysical UFO reality. In fact, the ET itself may be the spiritual embodiment of a metaphysical, etheric being that is evolving. They may be evolving in a different dimension, or they may possibly be evolving here on Earth.

There are trillions upon trillions of entities on Earth that are not human, and in my journeys I've seen a great variety of these types of evolutions. In fact, I think humans on Earth are quite rare when compared to all the other stuff that's here with us.

Do you believe in alien abduction?

I do. I think some of the abductions are etheric, out-of-body, and some of them may be literally physical as well, for people find themselves back in bed with grass cuttings and bruises, and x-rays have been taken of implants and so forth.

We may have a phenomenon whereby etheric beings of a dubious nature are mimicking the ET phenomena to grant themselves credibility with humans.

I'm a little bit worried about discovering alien abductions via hypnotic regression, because that is so open to imagination and the hypnotist leading the subject. So some of the abduction stories are obviously embellished. However, I can say categorically, from my own experience and investigations, that human beings are being tinkered with etherically, whether or not they are being physically transported to craft in the air.

How can people protect themselves from alien abduction?

Researchers such as Budd Hopkins have discovered some interesting facts. First, people who have been abused as children are more likely to be abducted, as they are more open psychically to being used. Second, the more you read or think about UFOs—the more you focus on them—the more likely they will appear in your life. You pull them into you by being fascinated by them. Third, if you are etherically damaged by emotions or drugs, or if you have a history of dabbling in black magic, your protection is diminished, and this also leaves you open.

So far there's only one protection that seems to work, and that is to leave the light on in your bedroom with a video camera playing all night, filming you while you're sleeping. The other thing I think ought to work but have not tried as yet, is to line your bed with lead. That might be a bit drastic but it's all trial and error at the moment. Copper wire strung all round the bed might also stuff 'em up. Try it.

It seems as if the number of UFO sightings is increasing. Do you think this is all building up to something?

There is something happening. In the early days of UFO sightings, there were only a few scattered reports from around the world, and of course many of the reports might well have had reasonable explanations. But now the phenomena is so pervasive, and our radar technology and ability to look into deep space is so much better than it used to be, that you'd be silly not to take notice of the mounting evidence. Over a million people saw the UFOs over Mexico City in 1991, and sightings worldwide are running at thousands per week.

Also, there is more of a worldwide perspective now, and suddenly we realize that the UFO thing is enormous. Sightings are running to hundreds of thousands annually, and if the people who say they've been abducted are to be believed, contact with these mysterious entities might be running in the millions. Just north of where I used to live in New Mexico is the highest concentration of cattle mutilations in the world. Hundreds have been taken over the last few years. Total estimates of animal mutilations worldwide, over the last 20 years, are placed at 300,000 so far.

Something big is happening. And we're soon going to find out what it is. There appears to be an enormous intrusion into human affairs. However, as we open up and become more technologically sophisticated, and as we start to think in transdimensional ways, those denizens of the other world that have been here all the time are appearing in our consciousness and in our world more and more.

We hear a lot about the "Grays," the small, skinny ETs with big heads and almond-shaped eyes. Do you think they are evil, or are they here to help us?

The Grays exhibit no obvious evil, or any obvious good. They show no emotion and give off a neutral energy. The nearest thing I have seen in the astral world to this non-energy are zombie types, and they are also neutral. The Grays have that same astral zombie feel to them. They don't really have a mind of their own; they are a projection or concoction of someone—or something—else's mind, like a phantom. I'm leaning toward the idea that under the big heads and buggy eyes of the Grays is a reptilian energy. Once or twice I have gotten a glimpse of something *behind* the Grays, and it looked like a reptile. It had yellow eyes with vertical black strips for pupils, like a snake's. Its energy was very dodgy. Maybe by projecting itself as a wimpy scrawny Gray, you can't really tell if it's satanic.

Anyway, all these beings are a part of all things, and so they should be loved, even if they are zombies or reptiles or satanic or whatever. Everyone and everything needs a helping hand toward God.

Do you have any theories on how the UFOs are able to travel such great distances?

To move from one star system to another, you'd have to be moving close to the speed of light, and even then it would take years. Any solid object moving at, say, almost 200,000 miles per second would be very vulnerable to damage. Even a speck of dust in space would destroy it. So if the UFOs are solid, they must have another way—either a way of bending space toward themselves so that distance is covered without much movement—that is, you bend space so a location comes and gets you, rather than you moving to it—or a technology that allows them to go into a nonsolid state while they are moving close to the speed of light so they can't be destroyed by debris.

However, the more likely scenario is that the UFOs have always existed in and around our planet, only in another dimension which they can blip in and out of. There are many correlations between the etheric world, the fairy kingdoms, and the UFOs. In those worlds/dimensions, shape-shifting is just a thought-form, and reality is not solid. However, the etheric world is a mid-state—not solid but not completely transparent either. A human can operate in the solid physical state and also in the etheric state; the etheric body can be moved around, in and out of the third dimension. So it's almost certain that there are other beings that can do the same thing. But maybe their ability to move around via the etheric is a lot more advanced than ours.

Now, if you found out you could move from your nonsolid or etheric dimension into the human 3-D world—and if you had an agenda which included using humans in some way—turning yourself into a flying saucer that performed marvelous feats would give everyone the impression that you were very evolved and very powerful. People would be scared of you, and they would give you their power. You could most likely do whatever you liked until people cottoned on to the fact that you're just a flying reptilian on a power trip, and a bit nasty to boot!

Do you believe the governments have secret information on UFOs and ETs?

Yes, I definitely do. Governments lie all the time. They cover up, confuse people, and feed us misinformation. However, if I were a higher spiritual being visiting from another galaxy, I certainly wouldn't give human governments my technology —any government that acquired such technology would wind up controlling the world—so I don't believe such a deal has been done.

There is ever-amounting evidence, however, that there are possibly alien bases underground in Puerto Rico, New Mexico, and Brazil. Whether or not these are set up through some treaty or collusion (however bizarre that may sound), I don't know. But the evidence is mounting so rapidly that I think we would be silly to imagine there isn't something going on, whether it's with governments' permission or not.

People say that governments are going to come clean and own up—I doubt it. I think at the very best they'll issue contradictions and confirmations and more contradictions, keeping everybody wondering. Just recently the American Air Force issued what it called its final statement on the Roswell crash, saying that it was definitely a weather balloon and that the bodies found there were, in fact, crash-test dummies. Of course nobody believes the government—which works as reverse psychology. By putting out a statement nobody will believe, you encourage people to make up their minds independently that the opposite is true. In other words, by saying that the Roswell crash was a balloon, you get everybody believing that it wasn't a balloon, and that in fact a spacecraft did crash in Roswell, New Mexico. Those are the kinds of tricks they're up to. However, I never worry much about what governments are doing because I've never been convinced that they're anything but completely stupid. The evolution of humanity will trot along to its own dictates, not the governments' or the United Nations.

What do you think the extraterrestrials want with us?

It's hard to say. It seems they're not here to conquer Earth, because if they were, they would have done it by now. Also, it doesn't seem like they're here to interfere with the evolution of humanity, though they may be using people for their own agenda.

If the ETs are from a higher civilization and are here to use, indoctrinate, and disempower humans, we're in trouble. However, it's not that different from what our media and government have been doing for years and years; feeding us loads of BS, manufacturing acquiescence and consent, and abducting our energy by stealing from our creative efforts. So the ETs could just be a manifestation of what's happening to our society already. All the more reason to take your power back, keep your head down, stay anonymous or hard to find, and if possible, move around a lot. That's how our lads stay safe.

It would seem to me that the extraterrestrials want us to know they're there, and they seem to be watching us. They're certainly watching the development of consciousness within human beings. Something very big is just about to happen. I believe it will change humanity's perception forever.

Chapter Eleven

WILDE ABOUT MYSELF

What is the most peculiar/frightening supernatural experience you have ever had?

I could probably make an entire tape consisting solely of my supernatural experiences. Perhaps I ought to do that one day. I'll pick a few in answer to your question, but they may not necessarily be the most frightening or the most amazing. They would just be those I remember.

One that comes to mind occurred in New Mexico during one of my *Warriors in the Mist* seminars. There was a point in the seminar when I got everybody into a trance state, and through a series of exercises, I would take them on a mini out-of-body experience. But rather than it being in the astral body, disconnected from the physical body, it was an OBE in the etheric. It was very spacey and weird.

At the end of the session, there is a point where I clap my hands, and 60 people stand up in their etheric bodies, leave their physical bodies in trance on the ground, and head for one corner of the tent. In that corner, reaching through me, they would grab a piece of information that I'd instructed them to get hold of. On this particular night as they came flying through me etherically, I blanked out. My mind just went "clunk clunk," and I wasn't there for a second. I was mentioning it to my friend Mike Vernon, who was at the back of the tent, and he said, "Did you know that when you clapped your hands and they went through, you disappeared?" And I said, "Well, it was really odd, because as they went through, I had this impression of not being there for a moment."

After the session, Mike and I sat outside having a drink and talking about the existence of other dimensions and spirit beings. I was telling him how I felt the presence of strange beings at the tent during the seminar. I decided to walk down the mountain. It was getting dark. The seminar tent was up about 11,000 feet, and it was about a 20-minute walk down to the ski lodge in the valley below. As I was walking down the hill, I noticed by some trees what seemed to me to be some etheric movement. I actually stopped, because I wondered for a second if it was an animal. There were no animals there that I could see.

I continued walking and became aware of a movement behind me. I thought it was odd, but I kept going. By now it was fairly dark. I was almost three-quarters of the way down the hill when I came upon a glowing ball right in the middle of the path. It was about one-and-a-half to two feet in circumference. It didn't glow *much*, but it definitely glowed. I stopped and looked at the ball, and I couldn't figure it out. The interesting thing was that I couldn't see through the ball, yet it had no physical solidity either. I made a step to the left, and the ball moved in front of me. I made a couple of wide steps to the right, and the ball came to the right. No matter which way I went, left or right, the ball moved with me. It wouldn't let me pass, and I wasn't keen on walking right into it. At this point I was still about six feet away from it, but I couldn't tell what it was.

In the end, I sat down on the side of the road and just watched it. It stayed there for a couple of minutes. Once the ball realized I wasn't going to get into an antagonistic situation with it, and that I was going to sit it out, it came off the center of the road, onto my side, about three yards in front of me, then it just gradually drifted down the hill and left the path clear for me. I wouldn't say it was a particularly frightening experience, but it was certainly interesting.

Another phenomenon I find fascinating is experiencing my personality disappear. I can probably illustrate this point best by describing how it occurred to me the first time. I was living in Sydney, Australia, with my second wife, Robyne, and my little boy, Sebastien. Sebastien used to come into my bed at night, and he would spin around and kick the way kids do and wake me up. So, often I would go into his bed.

On this particular night, I was asleep in his room, with the Ninja Turtle sheets and teddy bears and all that sort of stuff. I woke up at about three o'clock in the morning, sat up in the bed, and had no impression of my personality being present. There was no sense of "I." I wondered for a moment if I was actually asleep. I tapped my hand up against something to see if I was awake. One of the ways you can tell whether you're dreaming is whether or not reality looks incongruous or illogical. More often than not in dreams, progression from one act to another is oddly jerky or not synchronized. I could see that everything was proceeding normally, but I had no impression of a personality inside a physical body.

I walked into the bedroom where my wife and little boy were sleeping. I knew who they were, but I had no sense of attachment, no sense that they were part of my family. I walked through the house and continued to experience this very strange state of being in an infinite place. I was everywhere and nowhere and didn't have a personality, a sense of the "I" present inside the body. My first feeling was that it is extremely, supernaturally, incredibly weird. The first time it happened to me in Sydney I was really scared.

I went into the kitchen and got a drink, then went out onto a deck that overlooked Sydney Harbor, and took all my clothes off. Ever so gradually, after 20 minutes or so, the coldness of the night brought that sense of "I" back. I've had that disappearing personality experience happen to me various times since then.

Another memorable experience occurred when I was on a walk in the woods in Ireland sometime ago, and I went through a sort of near-death experience where I stepped into another world and looked back to our world. I had a feeling that the trees and people with me were not opaque. I could see through them. After that near-death experience, I had a sort of supernatural sense of the eternity of the spirit within. It felt like finding the Holy Grail. It's one of the most beautiful spiritual experiences I've ever had.

I've also had a few visions up the near-death tube. I found I could entrance myself, simulate a near-death sensation, and find the near-death tube. I've had maybe two or three hundred experiences where I visioned into these areas at the end of the near-death tube. On a few occasions, I had some really solid glimpses of the God Force. The enormity of that love and compassion, and the serenity of the God Force, is awe-inspiring. So they would also rank as major supernatural/metaphysical experiences that have really impacted me.

Where do you currently find yourself on your spiritual path?

I stopped giving seminars in the autumn of 1996. I wanted to take three years off in order to develop myself and come back with a whole new perception and awareness. What I discovered was that, in the razzmatazz of going out and traveling through 90 cities—talking about the God Force, dimensions, perceptions, the living spirit, the Light of God—one actually cuts oneself off from the teachings. It seems ludicrous, but that's what happens.

In the expediency and physical toughness of having to wake up every morning and go to the airport, fly to a city, appear at night, finish at midnight, wake up at 6A.M. to get on another plane, and so on, you're not in the spiritual world. You're not in the stillness. I would arrive at a hotel at eleven or noon, go into my room, close the curtains, and meditate for three or four hours before going on stage. But somehow that never really worked. It was just enough to sustain me day to day.

So, part of my spiritual journey is to pull back from talking about these dimensions, from having to be up on stage entertaining, shocking people, instructing them or just keeping them amused. Rather than talking about these inner worlds, it's sort of like walking through. I was amazed that the minute I stopped teaching, a huge door just opened up. It was always there and it was always available, but I couldn't walk through and perceive this other world while I had to be up on the stage hamming it up in the physical world.

So now, having walked through to that other place, the first few months have been a bit confusing, and I'm still settling with the whole idea. But, bit by bit, I know that walking through will create for me a new perception and a new teaching. I may take that teaching on the road and block myself off from the inner world for a bit, or I may just offer that teaching in the form of books, tapes, and my newsletter, and allow people to ponder it that way.

So we can expect to see new teachings in the coming years?

Yes, definitely. I've decided to take a little time off to really develop a consolidation of energy on the other side of the veil—the side that differentiates the physical world from the spiritual. I've straddled these two worlds for a very long time, and now I want to offer the methodology to others so they can do the same—quickly and easily, without having to go through years of trial and error, as I did. So I'll package all of that into a new teaching.

What are your latest projects?

I'm trying to put together a castle in which to reestablish the legend of Camelot. The idea came out of my *Warriors in the Mist* seminars, which I finished in '96. The idea that it is possible to create a new dimension within the evolution of this planet—one that takes people into the sanctuary, sensuality, and serenity of another world. However, in order to create that transdimensional energy, I need the right setting. So at the moment, I'm busying myself collecting the funds necessary to purchase a castle. When it's ready, I'll invite those people who wish to come. We'll open proceedings with a large banquet, and then take it from there.

You've taken a great interest in the legend of King Arthur and Camelot. (*Tolemac* is the word *Camelot* spelled backwards.) Do you think Camelot existed in real life, or was it just a metaphor?

Yes, I'm very keen on the legend of King Arthur and Camelot. My old teacher said that Camelot existed as a dimension. There is a dimension that I'm familiar with that I call "love's domain." I mention it briefly in the lyrics of *Heartland*, an opera I worked on with Tim Wheater. It's like entering a trance state while awake. In that trance state, life becomes extremely sensual, loving, and soft, and time becomes diffused and very spacious. You move inside a sense of being infinite inside a finite world. After a period of training, you could walk through from the physical world into love's domain and out the other side.

I've been in love's domain several times. I was in it for a three-day period with several other people, wandering around for about 22 hours a day. It's a place of extremes—extremes of energy, perception, and softness. It's a form of ecstasy. I'm not really sure how one enters the dimension of love's domain at will, but I aim to find out.

I have a feeling Camelot existed in love's domain. I also think it's a metaphor for a higher power, the Holy Grail, the honorable ideals of the knights and the ladies, the idea of magic and the power of Excalibur, and so on. But I think it was also a real place in another dimension. It wasn't necessarily a tangible place such as a castle, but it was a state of mind, a metaphysical dimension.

I've noticed that you've been focusing a lot on music since the release of the album, *Cecilia, Voice of the Feminine Spirit*, which I understand was very successful. Why are you now focusing on music?

My old teacher used to talk about dimensions that are beyond the mind, what I would call rotations in hyperspace. One of those he talked about was music of a celestial nature—music that is beyond the intellect and emotions, which, at an etheric level, has a violet color.

After I met the Norwegian soprano, Cecilia, I began thinking about the idea of creating a sound close to the music of the celestial worlds that I've heard in trance.

When you listen to a piece of music that has an ethereal violet nature, or that is even indigo or blue in its color, it carries you away from the three-dimensional and the mundane. It places your consciousness in a celestial world where information and healing energy flow. All my music has been geared toward reaching for this sacred space. You can hear the violet sound in a number of tracks on the first Cecilia album, especially in her rendition of *Amazing Grace*. Here and there you hear it on her second album, *Violet 19*. I'm currently working on several more albums with other bands and musicians, going for the "violet" sound.

Recently I've been in Ireland working with a band called Greenwood, and their first album will be called *Voice of the Celtic Myth*. It tells the story of the Tuatha de Danaan, the mythical gods of Ireland and their battles with the forces of darkness.

How did you come to make the album, *Cecilia, Voice of the Feminine Spirit*?

I met Cecilia, the Norwegian soprano, at one of my *Warrior's Wisdom* seminars. She said she could sing, so I asked her to get on the table and sing in a cafeteria, and she did. She sang *Amazing Grace*, and it was so beautiful, I thought, *Wow!* Then I got together with Tim Wheater, the New Age flautist, and a couple of other lads, and started stitching together some sounds, lyrics, and eventually songs for Cecilia to sing. The album did really well, and we now have a second album out called *Cecilia, Voice of Violet 19*. It's been fun and interesting, and I've learned a lot.

With your success in writing, seminars, and now music, are there any other avenues you would like to pursue—film or television, perhaps?

I'm quite interested in film, but I'm not interested in the people. My few brushes with Hollywood people didn't do much for me. I didn't care for all that self-promotion filmland thing. You get these people who talk in loud voices in restaurants, and they're always talking about what movie they're going to make for Disney or whatever. I found them rather flashy and arrogant, banal, egotistical, over-the-top, and flaky.

Television is okay. There was a time when I was trying to get a job as a television talk-show host. I did get quite close to the possibility. But the nearer I got to it, the more I saw that being the host of a TV show is like working for the post office. It's incredibly tick-tock. You roll along every day, you do the same thing, you have the same producers, the same floor assistants, the guests come along, you go home, and do it all again the next day. It's pure tick-tock.

The other thing about television that bothers me a hell of a lot, particularly American television, is that it's very strictly controlled. There is a real cap on what you can and can't say. You can't offend anyone. So television is dry-cleaned of any real spark. It has to fit the middle class, petty bourgeois, religious ideas of the nation. So I think TV would be really stifling.

Having said that, I do have a plan to make some simple documentaries in some sacred places. I've had the plan for several years, and never got the financing or wherewithal to make it. I was going to trot around various sacred sites and talk. For example, there's a dungeon in a castle I know of. Inside there are torture chambers with a rack and so on. Prisoners were shoved through a tiny hole in the ground into a minute cell covered by a metal grill. They had absolutely no room to move and were literally stuffed in and left there for years.

I thought of going to a place like that and making a documentary about, let's say, restriction. I could talk about the various forms of emotional, mental, physical, political, religious, and social restriction that we suffer. I would do it in a location like a dungeon where, pictorially, it would be easy to understand.

Do you have many close, personal friends?

I have a few people I'm really close to, and I love them deeply. But they're mostly people I have worked with over the years. When I was flying around and appearing in different cities, I had good friends and acquaintances all over the planet. But I'm like most people when it comes to close personal friends—you might have half a dozen or so. Then I have loads and loads of acquaintances I've worked with over the years who have my love and affection. So I do and I don't.

Who is the one person living today that you admire most in the world?

I'd like to cheat on this question slightly. There are a lot of artists, writers, and so on whose work I admire. But I don't know if any one particular person stands out. There are a lot of teachers in the New Age movement whom I admire for their success, such as Deepak Chopra, Tony Robbins, Wayne Dyer, and Louise Hay. They are all people who have created change in this world. I would say that really the group of people I admire most are the men and women at the forefront of quantum physics. I think it's through quantum physics that we're going to eventually discover the secrets to the universe. People like Hawkins and Penrose are characters I would admire because of their contribution to human understanding.

Why do some people call you "The Prince of Darkness"?

I haven't been called "The Prince of Darkness" for a long time. When I first went on the seminar circuit, a lot of the New Age was very fluffy, "standing in the white light" kind of stuff. I came along rather more biff-bang, and was rather crude and down-to-earth, and a bit more practical. What I did was very successful, and I think some teachers resented my success. They didn't like my brashness, or the fact that I was wooing their audiences away. I don't think I've ever been called the "Prince of Darkness" by anyone who considered themselves equal to, or better than me, only by those who felt they were inadequate. But everybody's entitled to their perception.

Have you ever considered writing your autobiography?

I have, and in fact I've actually started it. But I don't like autobiographies like, "I was born in so and so, then I went to Vienna, then I went to the university, then I married Harry," and so on. I find that very uninteresting and dull. Books like David Niven's *The Moon Is a Balloon* and the like are autobiographical in nature, but they're comedy books. I started an autobiographical comedy book sometime ago, and I've written about five chapters. One of these days when I have a minute, I'll finish it off. It's really the story of incidents in my life. Of course, traveling around the world, I've been in a lot of strange places and funny situations. So if I ever do an autobiography, that's what I'll do.

What's your favorite joke?

I think any joke is good if it makes you laugh. However, I always find that jokes have a low energy, because they are usually derogatory of self or others. I think the funniest comedy is where you can paint a picture with words, and people can follow along a storyline. That's the kind of humor I've always used on stage. I think jokes like, "Have you heard the one about the Irishman, Scotsman, and Englishman" are a little limp. I've never been keen on dirty jokes; I find them low energy and deprecating.

Do you have many happy memories of your childhood in Africa?

Some of the happiest memories of my life come from my childhood in Africa, because it was so free. Also, when I lived in Africa in the early '50s, many of the modern problems of today didn't exist. We didn't have TV, VCRs, and the media explosion that has created so much of the "dis-ease" in the planet. We lived with a childlike simplicity, where toys were simple things like a hoop and a stick, or a rubber tire on a rope hanging off a tree. It was a life of simplicity living in Africa in my younger years, and it was a time that I cherished—the simplicity of life, the solidity, the certainty of things.

What's your worst habit?

I suppose my worst habit is that I'm a bit of a dreamer. I've always held this Utopian view for the evolution of humanity, and often I've been mercilessly disappointed. But I still carry on this, perhaps naïve, dream. I believe in the Light, and I believe in goodness. Maybe in the short term, darkness and evil win, but in the long term I believe goodness will win. So I suppose my worst habit is my belief in it. But I was trained to believe.

In your album, *Cecilia, Voice of the Feminine Spirit*, one of the songs, "The Sacred Hum," has an interesting line: "I toiled and toiled and then I found the source of all eternal sound....It is a sacred hum." Can you tell us more about that song and what the words mean?

The sacred hum was an ancient teaching I learned about via a Taoist teacher. At the time of the winter solstice in a certain Taoist monastery, the hum was used to transport the monks/sages into an altered state of consciousness, or another world. As that hum begins to oscillate through the body, it creates very subtle, transdimensional changes.

At this time, I cannot tell you more about the hum. I'm currently working on defining the exact oscillation, and the precise pitch and nature of the hum, and I'm beginning to define it by experimentation. But I haven't finished yet, so I'll have to come back to you on this one. I feel it's pointless coming up with an extremely useful technique that may induce visions, out-of-body experiences, or create inspiration if one can't translate those ideas into simple terms ordinary people can understand. Most important for me, I don't like to teach things ordinary people can't do.

It always bugged me when wizards, sages, and holy men alluded to great powers and perceptions, and then ended with, "Your energy is too little to understand; these powers are beyond you, sit here cross-legged for another five incarnations and maybe, possibly, you'll get it." I like mysticism that's user-friendly, here and now, explainable in simple terms, and potentially do-able by ordinary people like myself.

I have more or less got the hum sorted out. I'm missing one component, but once I have that last part, I'll offer it in a simple format anyone can understand and use. Expect it some time before the end of this millennium.

If there was one thing you could change about yourself, what would it be?

I presume this question doesn't mean physically, because honestly I'd rather look like Tom Cruise than Stuart Wilde. But in relation to myself and my life, I really wouldn't change that much because, the way it is, is the way it is. I feel that each of us has to accept the way we find ourselves. I don't think we ever really stray very far from our destiny. I follow my destiny and feel fairly happy with it.

If you could go back and change one thing from your past, what would it be?

What is past is past, and to hanker to change things is a bit of a worthless exercise. I feel that I have followed my path strongly in this lifetime. Although I made some mistakes, when I look back at them years later, they weren't really mistakes. I could have chosen A or I could have chosen B, and I made my choice and that was it. So I don't think there are a lot of things I would change.

I left Africa when I was ten and went to an English boarding school, and I always considered that a great misfortune. Perhaps I could have stayed in Africa till I was 18 or so, but then my destiny may have been very different. Perhaps I could have been more disciplined in my 20s, when I did a lot of drinking and drugs and probably knocked 10 or 20 years off my life. But then again, I had a lot of visions, opened up my consciousness, and came upon a spiritual path as a result of going through those totally crazy years. So I don't think I'd change anything.

What is your first memory?

My first memory is of being in a baby carriage with my twin sister, Dee Dee, who's a dancer. I remember being down by a lake with her in the carriage, and I was in some sort of argument with her about the space in the carriage. I suppose we must have been about one-and-a-half or two. Weird but true.

How did you come to believe that life was not meant to be a struggle?

I came to the conclusion that life was never meant to be a struggle after studying Taoist texts. When you look at the Tao, it has a natural simplicity in the way it's worded, and of course the main teacher of the Taoist writers was nature.

In nature we see animals making an effort to give birth or making an effort to feed themselves, but you don't see struggle. The difference between struggle and effort is emotion. Struggle is effort laced with emotion. I don't believe our nature as humans is to struggle. I believe the ego places certain ideas in the mind to force us to strive to materialize its vision. This can create negative emotion and struggle if life doesn't immediately give the ego what it wants. Once you have control over the mind, struggle falls away automatically. Use the ebb and flow of nature as your teacher, and you'll soon see how it is free, for it is not a victim of emotions.

Your first book was *Miracles*. How long did it take you to write?

I wrote *Miracles* in seven hours. It was an amazing morning. I started writing at 5 A.M. and didn't stop until I finished the book at lunch time. Of course, later on I had to reread the book, edit it, and generally fix it up, but it flowed from start to finish in one sitting. No book that I have written since has been quite that easy. It's sold about 500,000 copies so far, and that's a little miracle in itself, for prior to that I had never written anything. I didn't even write home to mum.

What do you do when you want to relax?

I find it hard to relax in cities. At times during my life, I've had to live in cities, but I mostly prefer the country. I like the silence, and walking in the forest. I love to meditate out in nature. I enjoy watching the stars at night. I get my binoculars and telescope out, and I find that relaxing. But more than anything else, I read. I read endless books on cosmology, quantum physics, and that kind of stuff. I'm always probing for the answer to the great mystery. I'm sure one doesn't find the answer in books, but books are marvelous in that they help us along the journey; they help us to imagine, and they create the building blocks for a higher perception.

What's your favorite music?

My favorite music is the kind of music I write. That sounds awfully egotistical, but it's the truth. I like angelic and inspirational music—anything that expresses hope and inspiration. Here and there in the famous operas there are snippets of arias that are incredibly beautiful. But mostly I like soft angelic stuff that wafts the spirit up to higher ground.

If you had a time-machine, where would you go first?

I would very much like to go back into ancient history, just to get a feel for its rawness and earthiness. I'd like to go back to the time of the Romans and take a quick look at that. I'd particularly like to be in an army marching along with Alexander the Great, or someone like him. The other place I'd like to visit would be England in the Elizabethan era. I think it would be interesting to be inside one of those ale houses, smell their food, try their drinks, and feel that earthiness of being crammed into an ale house with a whole bunch of people before the invention of modern plumbing.

But after I'd whizzed around a few of those types of experiences in my time machine, the time I would really like to visit would be the prehistory of humanity. I'd like to go back to 10,000 B.C., when I believe there was a civilization on the Earth plane that was as evolved as we are today, if not more so. I'd love to go back and see if that were true. I'd even like to go further back to 60 million years ago and just have 10 or 15 minutes of wandering about looking for a few dinosaurs. I think that would be extremely cool, watching dinosaurs walking across the plains.

The other thing I'd like to do in my time machine is to zoom forward 500 or 1,000 years just to see whether humanity makes it or not. That would be fascinating because, as we become more technologically advanced, our planet is becoming more crowded and we're generating a huge crisis for ourselves. Also, we've got the atom bomb up our sleeve, so it's a possibility that in a thousand years' time there won't be anybody here. So if I could whiz forward in my time machine and take a look, that would be a whole bunch of fun.

Why do you call us heroic beings?

I think humanity is heroic because our intrinsic state is one of insecurity. We live in a finite body that can experience pain and anguish and all the unpleasant emotions that can come about when things go wrong in life. The heroism of our condition is in looking at life in a positive way, loving one another, and developing a relationship with God in spite of our insecurity and fear. The spirit that is deep within you came from a sacred place, a place more beautiful than any words could possibly describe. Inside that sacredness, that heritage of your original spiritual existence, are the roots of your return, your train ticket back to that sacred and holy place from which you came.

In 25 words or less, what do you see as your main goal in life?

To set myself free, to see life as heroic, and to help liberate other people.

ABOUT STUART WILDE

Author and lecturer **Stuart Wilde** *is one of the real characters of the self-help, human-potential movement. His style is humorous, controversial, poignant, and transformational. He has written 13 books, including those that make up the very successful Taos Quintet, which are considered classics in their genre. They are:* Affirmations, The Force, Miracles, The Quickening, *and* The Trick to Money Is Having Some. *Stuart's books have been translated into 12 languages.*

STUART WILDE INTERNATIONAL TOUR AND SEMINAR INFORMATION

For information on Stuart's latest tour and seminar dates in the USA and Canada,
contact:

White Dove International
P.O. Box 1000
Taos, NM 87571
(505) 758-0500 (phone)
(505) 758-2265 (fax)
Stuart's Website: **www.powersource.com/wilde**

ABOUT LEON NACSON

***Leon Nacson** was born in Alexandria, Egypt, to Greek parents. He is the founder and publisher of **The Planet** newspaper in Australia, a well-established publication that deals with environmental, healing, and personal development issues. He has also facilitated seminars and workshops throughout Australia for such notable individuals as Louise Hay, Wayne Dyer, Denise Linn, Shakti Gawain, Deepak Chopra, and Stuart Wilde.*

* * *

BY LEON NACSON

Aromatherapy for Meditation and Contemplation
(co-authored with Karen Downes and Judith White)

Aromatherapy for Lovers & Dreamers
(co-authored with Karen Downes and Judith White)

Cards, Stars, and Dreams

Deepak Chopra's World of Infinite Possibilities

Dyer Straight

I Must Be Dreaming

Dream Journal
and
Interpreting Dreams A–Z
(both available from Hay House in July 1999)

OTHER HAY HOUSE TITLES OF RELATED INTEREST

Books

Absolute Happiness, by Michael Domeyko Rowland

The Power Is Within You, by Louise L. Hay

A Spiritual Philosophy for the New World,
by John Randolph Price

Staying on the Path, by Dr. Wayne W. Dyer

Audios

The Heart of Spiritual Practice, by Jack Kornfield,
with Michael Toms

How to Get What You Really, Really, Really, Really Want
(six-tape audio program),
by Wayne W. Dyer and Deepak Chopra

Meditations for Manifesting, by Wayne W. Dyer

The New Millennium, by Jean Houston,
with Michael Toms

Spiritual Principles (four-tape set),
by Marianne Williamson

* * *

We hope you enjoyed this Hay House book.
If you would like to receive a free catalog featuring additional Hay House books and products, or if you would like information about the Hay Foundation, please contact:

Hay House, Inc.
P.O. Box 5100
Carlsbad, CA 92018-5100

(760) 431-7695 or **(800) 654-5126**
(760) 431-6948 (fax) or **(800) 650-5115 (fax)**

Please visit the Hay House Website at: **www.hayhouse.com**

* * *